CW00726270

CHRIST AND
HUMAN SO

CHRIST AND THE HUMAN SOUL

RUDOLF STEINER

Four lectures given at Norrköping,
from 12th to 16th July, 1914

RUDOLF STEINER PRESS
LONDON

First English Edition 1927
Second edition 1956 (revised by M. Cotterell)
Third edition 1972 (revised by C. Davy)
Fourth edition 1984

Translated from shorthand reports unrevised by the lecturer. In the Complete Edition of the works of Rudolf Steiner the volume containing the original German text (together with the texts of other lectures) is entitled: *Christus und die menschliche Seele. Über den Sinn des Lebens. Theosophische Moral. Anthroposophie und Christentum.* (Bibl. No. 155). This English edition is published in agreement with the Rudolf Steiner Nachlassverwaltung, Dornach, Switzerland.

No part of this book may be reproduced in any form or by any means without the prior permission of the copyright holder, Rudolf Steiner Press, 38 Museum Street, London WC1A 1LP. All rights reserved.

© Rudolf Steiner Press, London 1972

British Library Cataloguing in Publication Data

Steiner, Rudolf
   Christ and the human soul.—4th ed.
   1. Christianity   2. Anthroposophy
   I. Title   II. Christus und die menschliche Seele. *English*
   200   BP595

   ISBN 0-85440-013-3

Printed and bound in Great Britain at
The Camelot Press Ltd, Southampton

THE PUBLICATION OF LECTURES HELD BY RUDOLF STEINER

The foundation of anthroposophically orientated Spiritual Science is laid in the works which were written and published by Rudolf Steiner (1861–1925). At the same time Steiner held numerous lectures and courses both for the general public and for Members of the Theosophical (later Anthroposophical) Society in the years between 1900 and 1924. It was not his original wish to have these lectures published which were without exception of a spontaneous nature and conceived as "oral communications not intended for print". However, after an increasing number of incomplete and erroneous listeners' transcripts had been printed and circulated, he found it necessary to have the notes regulated. He entrusted this task to Marie Steiner von Sivers. She was made responsible for the choice of stenographers, the supervision of their transcripts and the necessary revision of texts before publication. As Rudolf Steiner was only in a very few instances able to correct the notes himself his reservation in respect of all publications of his lectures must be taken into account: "Errors occurring in transcripts which I myself have been unable to revise will just have to be tolerated."

In Chapter 35 of his autobiography, Rudolf Steiner expounds on the relationship between his lectures for Members which were initially only circulated internally and his public writings. The relevant text is printed at the end of the book. What is expressed there also applies to the lecture courses directed towards a restricted audience already familiar with the principles of Spiritual Science.

After Marie Steiner's death (1867–1948) the editing of a "Complete Works of Rudolf Steiner" was commenced according to her directions. This book constitutes a part of this complete edition.

CONTENTS

for the whole cosmic order when their forces operate on their legitimate level. Judgments which hold good for the physical plane must not be supposed to hold good for the higher worlds. Christ a Being of the kingdom of Heaven, not of the kingdom of the Earth. Individual sin is not exempt from karmic justice, but Christ blots out from Earth evolution as a whole the debt and objective consequences of sin and guilt. The meaning of the "forgiveness of sins".

Lecture 4   60

Truths in themselves contain life-force. Christ became related to death because evolution of the universe made it necessary that a God of the upper worlds should be leader of Earth-evolution. The four ethers. Christ came from regions closed to man as a result of the Luciferic temptation: from the regions of the Music of the Spheres (chemical ether) and of Cosmic Life (life-ether). These regions were to be restored to man through the coming of Christ to the Earth. The meaning of the "Resurrection of the body". The Earth period will be followed by the Jupiter period, when two races, the good and the evil, will differentiate themselves. A Venus-existence will follow that of Jupiter, and again there will be an adjustment through the further evolution of the Christ-consciousness.

LECTURE 1

Let me first extend to you my heartfelt greetings. Friends in Norrköping have expressed the wish that on this occasion I should take a theme concerning that Being who in the realm of spiritual science is above all else near to us—the Christ Being. I have tried to meet this wish by undertaking to speak about the coming to life of the Christ Being in the human soul and the significance of this. We shall thus have the opportunity to speak of the most human and intimate significance of Christianity from the standpoint of spiritual science.

Let us consider the human soul. In the sense of spiritual science we have a short word which, although it does not embrace all that the expression "human soul" signifies for us, points to something which for us men of Earth fills and permeates the soul element to its farthest limits—we have the short word "I". In so far as we are men of Earth, our ego-being reaches as far as does our soul-nature. You know that by the name "I", or ego, we denote one of the four most immediate principles of man. We speak, in the first instance, of four members or principles of the human being—the physical body, the etheric body, the astral body and the ego. And in order to have the starting-point for what we shall be considering in these lectures, we need recall only one thing: we do not regard the laws and the living essence of the physical body of man as explicable in terms of our present earthly environment.

We know that if we want to understand the physical human

body we must go back to the three preceding embodiments of our Earth—the Saturn, Sun and Moon periods. In a remote, primordial past, during the Saturn embodiment, the germ of the physical body was already laid down. During the Sun embodiment the foundation of the etheric body was laid down; and during the Moon embodiment that of the astral body. In reality our Earth-evolution, in all its phases and in all its epochs, is none other than that which enables the ego to fulfil its whole being. We can say that just as the physical body had reached a significant stage of its evolution at the end of the Saturn period, the etheric body at the end of the Sun period, and the astral body at the end of the Moon period, so at the end of the Earth period our ego will have reached a significant point in its evolution.

We know that our ego develops through three soul members or principles, through the sentient soul, the intellectual or mind-soul, and the spiritual or consciousness-soul. All the worlds that come within the compass of these three soul members are also concerned with our ego. In the course of our Earth-evolution these three soul members first prepared for themselves the three external bodily members—the physical body, the etheric body and the astral body—through long Earth periods. In successive post-Atlantean epochs of civilisation the three soul principles developed further, and in future Earth periods they will again adapt themselves to the astral, etheric and physical bodies, so that the Earth can be prepared to pass over to the Jupiter evolution.

If we take the expression comprehensively enough, we might also speak of man's Earth-evolution as his soul evolution. One could say that when the Earth began, the soul element also began, in conformity with law, to bestir itself in man. At first it began to work on the external sheaths, then it developed its own being, and from then onward it begins again to work on the external sheaths in order that preparation may be made for the Jupiter evolution.

We must keep before our mind's eye what man is meant to become in his soul during the Earth evolution. He is to become what may be designated by the word "personality". This personality needs in the first place what may be called "free will". But it needs also, on the other side, the possibility of finding within itself the way to the divine in the world. On the one side free will, the possibility of choosing between the beautiful and the ugly, the good and the evil, the true and the false; on the other side, the laying hold of the divine so that the divine penetrates into the soul and we know ourselves to be inwardly filled with it. Such are the two goals of man's evolution on the Earth; and to aid him in reaching them he has received two religious gifts. One of these gifts is destined to lay down in the human soul those forces which lead to freedom, to the capacity for distinguishing between the true and the false, the beautiful and ugly, the good and bad. And another religious gift had to be given to man during his Earth evolution in order that there might be laid in his soul the seed through which the soul can feel united to the divine within itself.

The first religious gift comes to meet us at the beginning of the Old Testament as the great picture of the Temptation and the Fall.

The second religious gift comes to us from all that the Mystery of Golgotha signifies.

The Temptation and the Fall have to do with the implanting of freedom in man, the gift of being able to distinguish between good and bad, beautiful and ugly, true and false. The

Mystery of Golgotha points to the possibility of man's soul finding again the path to the divine, of knowing that the divine can flash up within it and penetrate it. These religious gifts include everything that is most important in the Earth evolution—everything proceeding from the Earth evolution that the soul can experience in its uttermost depths, everything associated most profoundly with the being and becoming of the human soul. How far is there a connection between these two religious gifts and the being and becoming of the human soul—its inner experience?

I do not want to put these matters before you in an abstract way, so I will start from a perfectly concrete element, from a certain scene in the Mystery of Golgotha as it stands before our eyes in historical tradition and has impressed itself—and should indeed have impressed itself even more—on the hearts and souls of mankind. Let us assume that we have in Christ Jesus that Being of whom we have often spoken in the course of our lectures. Let us assume that in Christ Jesus we have before our spiritual eyes that which must appear to humanity as the most important fact in the whole universe. And then let us set in contrast to this feeling the outcry, the fury, of the enraged multitudes in Jerusalem at the time of the condemnation before the crucifixion. Let us observe that the High Court of Jerusalem held it above all things necessary to question Christ Jesus as to His relationship with the divine, as to whether He claimed to be the Son of God. And let us bear in mind that the High Court held such a claim to be the greatest blasphemy that Christ Jesus could have uttered.

An historical scene is there before us—a scene in which the people cry out and clamour for the death of Christ Jesus. And now let us try to picture to ourselves what this shouting and rage signified historically. Let us ask: What ought these people to have recognised in Christ Jesus? They ought to have recognised that Being who gives meaning and significance to Earth life. They ought to have recognised that Being who had to accomplish the deed without which Earth humanity cannot find the way back to the divine. They ought to have understood that humanity has no significance apart from this Being. Men would have to strike out from the evolution of the Earth the word "man" if they wished to strike out the Christ Event. Now let it come home to us that this multitude condemned and were enraged against the Being who actually makes man Man upon the Earth; who is destined to give to the Earth its goal and purpose. What does this mean? Surely it means that in those who in Jerusalem at that time ranked as the representatives of human knowledge concerning the true being of man, the knowledge of man was obscured. They had no knowledge of what man is, what his mission on the Earth is to be. We are told nothing less than that humanity had reached a point where it had lost itself, where it had condemned that which gives purpose and significance to the Earth-evolution. And out of the cries of the enraged multitude could be heard, not the words of wisdom, but of folly: "We do not wish to be Man, rather do we wish to cast away from us that which gives us any further meaning as Man."

When we reflect on all this, the relation of man to sin and guilt—in the sense of Pauline Christianity—assumes a different aspect. Man, in the course of his evolution could fall into sin which he was not himself able to wash away; that is what St. Paul means. And in order to make it possible for man to be cleansed of sin and debt, Christ had to come to the Earth. That is St. Paul's view. If this view requires any evidence, it is there in the fury and clamour of those who cried "Crucify Him!" For this implies that the people did not know what they themselves were to be on the Earth; they did not know that it was the aim of their earlier evolution to veil their being with darkness.

Here we come to what may be spoken of as the preparation of the human soul for the Christ Being. Through what it is able to experience within itself, the soul feels, even though it may not be able to express it in words: "Since the very beginning of the Earth I have developed in such a way that through what I possess in my own being I cannot fulfil the aim of my evolution. Where is there anything to which I can cling, which I can take into myself and with it reach my goal?" To feel as if the human being extends far beyond anything that the soul can achieve through its own strength by reason of its evolution on the Earth hitherto—such is the Christian attitude or mood of preparation. And when the soul finds that which it must recognise as essentially bound up with its being—but for the attainment of which it could not find the power within itself—when the soul finds that which bestows this power, it finds the Christ. The soul then develops its connection with the Christ, saying to itself: "At the very beginning of the Earth a certain nature was pre-ordained for me; in the course of Earth-evolution my true nature has been darkened, and when now I look into this darkness I feel that I lack the power to bring my true nature to fulfilment. But I turn my spiritual gaze upon the Christ, who gives me this power." On the one hand the human soul feels this lack, and on the other hand it feels the approach of Christ and stands as if in a direct personal relationship to Him. The soul seeks Christ and knows that it cannot find Him if He does not give Himself to humanity through human evolution, if He does not approach from outside.

There is a well-known Christian Church Father who was

not afraid to speak of the Greek philosophers, Heracleitos, Socrates and Plato, as Christians who lived before the founding of Christianity. Why does he do this? As we know, the doctrines professed today obscure much of what was at first an illuminating Christian teaching. St. Augustine himself said: "All religions have contained something of the truth, and the element of truth in all religions is what is Christian in them, before there was a Christianity in name." St. Augustine dared to say that. Nowadays many a man would be regarded as a heretic if he were to say something similar within certain Christian congregations.

We shall most readily understand what this Church Father wished to convey, when he called the old Greek philosophers Christians, by endeavouring to enter into the feeling of those souls who in the first Christian centuries tried to determine their personal relationship to the Christ. These souls did not think of Christ as having had no relation to the Earth evolution before the Mystery of Golgotha. The Christ has always been concerned with the evolution of the Earth. Through the Mystery of Golgotha, however, His task, His mission, in the Earth-evolution was changed. It is not Christian to seek Christ in the evolution of the Earth only since the Mystery of Golgotha. True Christians know that Christ has always been connected with the evolution of the Earth.

Let us now turn to the Jewish people. Did the Jews know Christ? I am not asking whether the Jewish people knew the name of Christ or if they were conscious of all I have to say to you; I am asking whether those who really understand Christianity are justified in saying: "Judaism had Christ; Judaism knew Christ." It is possible to have some person near one and to see his external form without being able to recognise or value truly his essential being, because one has not risen to real knowledge of him. In the true Christian sense, ancient Judaism had Christ, only it did not recognise Him in His true being. Is it Christian to speak in this way? It is indeed Christian, as truly as it is Pauline.

Where was Christ for ancient Judaism? It is said in the Old Testament that when Moses led the Jews out of Egypt into the wilderness, a pillar of cloud went before them by day and a pillar of fire by night. It is said that the Jews passed through the sea, that the sea parted in order that they might pass through, while behind them the Egyptians were drowned, for the sea closed in on them. It is also said that the Jews murmured because they had no water, but at the command of God Moses was able to strike a rock with his staff so that water poured forth for the Jews to drink. Moses led the Jews, he himself being led by God. Who was the God of Moses? We will in the first instance allow Paul to answer. In the First Epistle to the Corinthians (X, 1–4); we read: "Moreover, brethren, I would not that ye should be ignorant how that all our fathers were under the cloud" (he means the pillar of fire) "and all passed through the sea and all were baptised unto Moses in the cloud and in the sea . . . and all drank of the spiritual Rock that followed them, and that Rock was Christ." Thus who was it, according to Paul, who led the Jews and who spoke with Moses? Who was it who caused water to flow out of the rock and who turned away the sea from the path of the Jews? Only those who wish to declare that Paul was no Christian would dare pronounce it unchristian to see Christ in the guiding God of the Old Testament, in the Lord of Moses.

In the Old Testament there is a passage which must, I think, present great difficulties for all who reflect more deeply. It is a passage to which anyone who does not read the Old Testament thoughtlessly, but who wants to understand its connections, will return again and again. ''What may this passage mean?'' he asks himself. The passage (Numbers, XX, 11–12) is as follows: ''And Moses lifted up his hand. and with his rod he struck the rock twice; and the water came out abundantly, and the congregation drank, and their beasts also. And the Lord spake unto Moses and Aaron: Because ye believed me not, to sanctify me in the eyes of the children of Israel, therefore ye shall not bring this congregation into the land which I have given them.''

Take this passage in its context in the Old Testament. When the people murmured, the Lord commanded Moses to strike the rock with a staff: Moses struck with his staff on the rock, and water flowed out; everything that the Lord commanded took place through Moses and Aaron, and yet, directly after this, we are told the Lord reproved Moses—if it is a reproof— for not having believed in Him. What does it mean? Turn to all the commentaries on this passage and try to understand it with their aid. You will then understand it as one understands a great deal in the Bible—really not at all—for behind this passage a great mystery is hidden. It is this: He who led Moses, who appeared to Moses in the burning bush, He who led the people through the wilderness and caused water to flow out of the rock, He was the Lord, Christ! But the time was not yet come; Moses himself did not recognise Him; Moses thought He was another. This is what is meant by Moses not having believed in Him who had commanded him to strike the rock with his staff.

How did the Lord—Christ—appear to the Jewish people? We are told that by day it was in a pillar of cloud and by night in a pillar of fire—and by His dividing the waters for their safety . . . and many other things we can read in the Old

Testament. In phenomena of cloud and fire, in the air, in the elemental events of nature He was active, but never once did it occur to the ancient Jews to say to themselves: That which appears in the pillar of cloud and in the pillar of fire, that which worked wonders such as the parting of the waters, appears also in its purest original form in the human soul. Why did this never occur to the ancient Jews? Because, owing to the course taken by human evolution, the soul of man had lost the power to feel its deepest being within itself. Thus the Jewish soul could look into nature; it could allow the glory of the phenomena of the elements to work upon it; everywhere it could divine the existence of its God and Lord; but directly within itself, as the Jewish soul then was, it could not find Him.

There in the Old Testament we have the Christ. There He worked, but men did not recognise Him. How did the Christ work? Do we not see how He worked when we read through the Old Testament? The most significant thing Moses had to impart to his people through the mouth of Jahve was the Ten Commandments. He had received them out of the power of the elements from which Jahve spoke to him. Moses did not descend into the depths of his own soul; he did not ask in lonely meditation: "How does God speak in my own heart?" He went up the mountain and through the power of the elements the divine Will revealed itself to him. Will is the fundamental note of the Old Testament: this is often spoken of as the Law. Will works through the evolution of humanity and is expressed in the Decalogue, the Ten Commandments. The God proclaimed his Will to man through the elements. Will holds sway in the Earth evolution. That is really the purport of the Old Testament, and the Old Testament, accordingly, calls for man's submission to this Will.

If we hold all this before our souls, we can sum it up by saying: The will of the Lord was given to men; but men did not know the Lord; they knew not the divine in such a way as to connect it with their own human souls.

Now let us turn from the Jews to the heathen. Did the heathen have Christ? Is it Christian to say of the heathen that they also had Christ? The heathen had their Mysteries. Those initiated in the Mysteries were brought to the point where their souls passed out of their bodies; the tie connecting body and soul was loosened; and when the soul was outside the body, it perceived in the spiritual world the secrets of existence. Much was connected with these Mysteries; much varied knowledge came to the candidates for Initiation in the Mysteries. But when we investigate what was the highest that the disciple of the Mysteries could receive into himself, we find that it consisted in the fact that outside the body he was placed before the Christ. As Moses was placed before Christ, so in the Mysteries was the disciple placed with his soul, outside his body, before Christ.

Christ was there for the heathen also, but for them he was there only in the Mysteries. He revealed Himself to them only when the soul was out of the body. Christ was there for the heathen, even if among them there was as little recognition of this Being as Christ as there was among the Jews of that Being of whom we have just spoken and before whom the disciples of the Mysteries were placed.

The Mysteries were instituted for the heathen. Those who were fit and ready were admitted into the Mysteries. Through these Mysteries Christ worked upon the pagan world. Why did He work thus? Because the soul of man, in its development since the beginning of the Earth, had lost the inherent power to find its true essence through itself. This true being

17

had to reveal itself to the soul of man when the soul was unhampered by the bonds of human nature; when, that is, it was not bound up with the body. Hence Christ had to lead men by means of the fact that as initiates of the Mysteries they were as though divested of their human nature. Christ was there for the heathen too! He was their leader in the Mysteries. For never could man have said: "When I develop my own powers, then I can find the meaning and purport of the Earth." This meaning was lost, obscured in darkness. The forces of the human soul had been pressed down into regions too deep for the soul of itself, through its own powers, to be able to realise the meaning of the Earth.

When we allow what was given in the pagan Mysteries to the disciples and candidates for Initiation to work upon us, it proves to be Wisdom. To the Jews was given Will, through the Law; to the disciples of the pagan Mysteries was given Wisdom. But if we look at the characteristics of this pagan Wisdom, can we not express it by saying: If he did not leave his body when he was a pupil of the Mysteries, the Earth-man could not, through Wisdom alone, recognise his God as such. As little through Wisdom as through Will could the divinity reveal itself to men. Indeed, we find an injunction that resounds most wonderfully through Greek antiquity, like a powerful demand upon mankind. At the entrance to the shrine of the Mysteries of Apollo stood the words, "Man, know thyself!" What are we told by the fact that these words, "Man, know thyself!" stood at the entrance to the sanctuary, like a summons to mankind? We are told that nowhere outside the sanctuary, where man remains what he has become since the beginning of the Earth, can he fulfil the commandment "Know thyself!" He must become something more than man; he must loosen in the Mysteries the ties which bind the soul to the body, if he is to know himself. These words, standing like a powerful demand before the Apollonian sanctuary, point to the fact that darkness had fallen upon humanity—in other words, that God could be reached through Wisdom as little as he could directly reveal himself as Will.

Even as the individual human soul feels that it cannot bring forth within itself the forces which impart to it the purport of the Earth, so do we see the human soul at such a stage of development among the Jews that even Moses himself, their leader, did not recognise who was leading him. Among the heathen we see that the demand ''Know thyself'' could be fulfilled only in the Mysteries, because man, as he had developed in the course of the evolution of the Earth, was unable with his connection of body and soul to unfold the power whereby he could know himself. The words ''Not through Will and not through Wisdom is God to be known'' sound to us from those ages. Through what, then, was God to be known?

We have often characterised the essential nature of the point of time when Christ entered into the evolution of Earth-humanity. Let us now consider exactly what it means when it is said that a certain darkening of the soul of man had set in, that the divine could be revealed neither through Will nor through Wisdom. What is the real meaning of this?

People speak of so many relationships between the human and the divine. They often speak of the relationship between the human and the divine, and of the meaning which the human has within the divine, in such a way that it is impossible to differentiate between the relation of the human to the divine, or of anything else earthly to the divine. Today we find again and again that philosophers want to rise to the divine through pure philosophy. But through pure philosophy one cannot rise to the divine. Certainly by means of it man does come to feel that he is bound up with the universe and to know that the human being must, in some way or other, be bound up with the universe at death; but how and in what manner he is thus connected with the universe he cannot know through pure philosophy. Why not? If you take the whole meaning of what we have considered today, you will be able to say to yourselves: What is at first revealed to the soul of earthly man between birth and death is too weak to perceive anything that transcends the earthly, that leads to the divine-spiritual. In order to make this quite clear to ourselves, let us investigate the meaning of immortality.

In our day many people no longer have any knowledge of the real meaning of human immortality. Many today speak of immortality when they can merely admit that the being of the human soul passes through the gate of death and then finds some place or other in the universal All. But every creature does that. That which is united with the crystal passes over into the universe when the crystal is dissolved; the plant that fades passes into the universe; the animal at death passes over into the universe. For man, it is different. Immortality has a meaning for man only if he can carry his consciousness through the gate of death. Think of an immortal human soul that was unconscious after death; such immortality would have absolutely no meaning. The human soul must carry its consciousness through the gate of death if it is to speak of its immortality. Because of the way in which the soul is united to the body, it cannot find anything in itself of which it can say, "I carry that consciously through death", for human consciousness is enclosed between birth and death; it reaches only as far as death. The consciousness that belongs at first to

the human soul extends only as far as death. Into this consciousness there shines the divine Will, for example in the
Ten Commandments. Read in the Book of Job as to whether
this illumination could stimulate man's consciousness to such
a point that it might say to itself: "I pass as a conscious being
through the gate of death." What a challenge to us there is in
the words spoken to Job: "Reject God and die!" We know
that he was uncertain whether he would pass with consciousness through the gate of death. And let us set beside this
the Greek saying which gives expression to the dread felt by
the Greeks in the face of death: "Better a beggar in the upper
world than a king in the realm of the shades." Here we have
from paganism, also, a testimony to the uncertainty felt by
man concerning his immortality. And how uncertain many
people are even today. All those people who say that man,
when he goes through the gate of death, passes into the
universal All and is united with some universal being or other,
take no heed of what the soul must ascribe to itself if it is to
speak of its immortality.

We need only pronounce one word, and we shall recognise
the attitude that man must take up with regard to his
immortality. The word is Love. All that we have said concerning the word immortality we can now connect with what
is denoted by Love. Love is not anything that we appropriate
to ourselves through the Will; or anything that we appropriate to ourselves through Wisdom. Love dwells in the realm
of the feelings. We must admit to ourselves that the human
soul would fall short of its true nature if it were unable to be
filled with love. Yes, when we penetrate into the nature of
the soul, we realise that our human soul would no longer be a
human soul if it could not love. But let us now suppose that
on passing through the gate of death we lost our human

21

individuality and were united with some universal divinity. We should then be within this divinity; we should belong to it. Love would have no meaning if we were within the Godhead. If we could not carry our individuality through death, we should in death have to lose love, for in the moment that individuality ceased, love would cease. One being can love another only if the other is separate from himself. If we are to carry our love of God through death, we must carry with us that which kindles love within us—our individuality.

If the meaning of the Earth was to be brought to man, information concerning his immortality had to be given him in such a way that his nature would be thought of as inseparable from love. Neither Will nor Wisdom can give man what he needs; only Love can give it to him. What was it, then, that became darkened in the course of man's evolutionary path on Earth? Take the Jews or take the heathen: their consciousness of anything beyond death had been darkened. Between birth and death—consciousness; beyond death and beyond birth—darkness; of their bodily consciousness nothing more remained. "Know thyself!"—at the entrance of the Greek Mysteries, stood this most holy demand of the sanctuary upon mankind. Man could only answer: "If I remain bound to my body with my soul, as is the way with a man of Earth, I cannot recognise in myself an individuality which could love beyond death. I cannot do it." The knowledge that man can love as an individuality beyond death—this is what had been lost for man.

Death is not merely the cessation of the physical body. Only a materialist can say that. Suppose that throughout every hour of life in the body man's consciousness were such that he knew what lies beyond death as certainly as he knows today that the sun will rise on the morrow and take its journey across the heavens. Then death would have no sting for him; death would not be what we call death; he would know in the body that death is only a phenomenon leading from one form to another. Paul did not understand by "death" the cessation of the physical body; by "death" he understood the fact that consciousness extends only as far as death, and that man, in so far as he was united with the body in the existence of that period, could, within his body, extend his consciousness only as far as death. Wherever Paul speaks of death, we might add: "Lack of consciousness beyond death."

What did the Mystery of Golgotha give to man? Was it a series of natural phenomena, a pillar of cloud, a pillar of fire, that stood before humanity with the Mystery of Golgotha? No! A man, Christ Jesus, stood before men. With the Mystery of Golgotha did any event drawn from the mysterious realms of nature take place—did a sea divide so that the people of God could go through? No! A man stood before men; a man who made the lame to walk and the blind to see. By a man were these things done.

The Jew had to look into nature when he wanted to see him whom he called his divine Lord. Now it was a man who could be seen. Of a man it could be said that God dwelt in him. The pagan had to be initiated; his soul had to be withdrawn from his body in order that he might stand before the Being who is the Christ. On the Earth he had been unable to divine the Christ; he could know only that the Christ was outside the Earth. But He who had been outside the Earth came down to Earth, took on a human body.

In Christ Jesus there stood as man before men that Being who had formerly stood in the Mysteries before the soul that was liberated from the body. And what came to pass through this? It was the beginning of the course of events whereby the powers that man had lost ever since the start of the Earth evolution—the powers which assured him of his immortality—were restored to him through the Mystery of Golgotha. The overcoming of death on Golgotha gave birth to the forces which could rekindle in the soul the powers it had lost. And the path of man through Earth evolution will henceforth be this: Inasmuch as he takes the Christ more and more into himself, he will discover within himself the power which can love beyond death, so that he will be able to stand before his God as an immortal individuality. Therefore, only since the Mystery of Golgotha has it become true to say: "Love God above all, and thy neighbour as thyself."

Will was given from out of the burning thorn-bush; Will was given through the Ten Commandments. Wisdom was given through the Mysteries. But Love was given when God became man in Christ Jesus. And the assurance that we can love beyond death, that by means of the powers won back for our souls a community of Love can be founded between God and man and all men among one another—the guarantee for that proceeds from the Mystery of Golgotha. In the Mystery of Golgotha the human soul has found what it had lost from the primal beginning of the Earth, in that its forces had become ever weaker and weaker.

Three forces in three members of the soul: Will, Wisdom, Love! In this Love the soul experiences its relation to Christ.

I wanted to bring these things before you from a certain aspect. Whatever may have seemed aphoristic in the explanations given today will find its context later on. But I believe we can inscribe deeply in our souls that progress in the knowledge of Christ is a real gain for the human soul, and that when we consider the relationship of the human soul to

Christ, it again becomes clear to us how before the Mystery of Golgotha there was a veil, as it were, between the human soul and Christ; how this veil was broken by the Mystery of Golgotha, and how we can say with truth: "Through the Mystery of Golgotha a cosmic Being flowed into Earth-life, a super-earthly Being united Himself with the Earth."

We shall speak in the following lectures of all that the human soul, with Christ, can experience within itself.

LECTURE 2

As we live through the day and realise all that we owe to the Sun, and to what extent the tasks of life are connected with the sunlight, we forget that through the whole pleasure and satisfaction we derive from the sunlight there runs the thread of sure knowledge that on the following morning, after we have rested through the night, the Sun will rise again. This is a token of the confidence that lives in our soul—confidence in the lasting reality of the world-order. We may not always consciously realise it, but if asked, we should certainly answer in this sense. We devote ourselves to our work to-day because we know that the fruits of our work are assured for to-morrow; that after the night's rest the Sun will reappear, and the fruits of our labour will ripen.

We turn our eyes to the Earth's covering of plants; we admire its display; we know the world-order ordains that the plants and fruits for next year will arise from the seeds of this year. If asked why we live on with such a sense of security, we should reply that the reality of the world-order seems to us assured; we feel certain that from the ripening of the old seeds a new flowering will emerge into full reality.

But if we are thinking of this kind of reassurance from external reality, there is something in face of which we need a support. It is something of quite special significance for our soul-life. And only one phrase need be uttered—"our ideals"—to make us feel the need for assurance, since to those who truly think and feel it will be obvious that the

26

phrase carries no such assurance in itself. When we think and feel in a higher sense, our ideals belong to those things that are more important to our souls than external reality. It is our ideals which fire our souls, and in many connections make life valuable and precious. And when we look at the assured reality of external life, we are often troubled by the thought: does this reality include anything that guarantees the most precious thing in life—the realisation of our ideals?

Innumerable conflicts in the human soul proceed from the fact that people doubt more or less strongly in the realisation of their ideals, although it is precisely on this that they would like to rely with every fibre of their being. We need only consider the world of the physical plane in an unprejudiced way and we shall find innumerable human souls passing through the hardest, bitterest conflicts because they are unable to bring to fulfilment their cherished ideals. For we cannot conclude from the course of evolution that our ideals in life will prove to be the seeds of a future reality in the same way as the plant-seeds of this year foretell next year's flowering. These plant-seeds, we know, bear within them a potential which next year will yield a manifest reality on the widest scale. But if we consider our ideals, we may indeed cherish the belief that they will have some significance, some value for life; but certainty in the same sense we cannot have. As human beings we should like our ideals to be the seeds of a later future, but we look in vain for anything that can give them assured reality. When we look at the physical plane, we find that our souls, with their idealism, are often in a state of despair.

Let us pass from the world of the physical plane into the world of the occult, the world of hidden spirituality. A man who has become a spiritual seer learns to know souls in the period through which they have to pass between death and a new birth, and it is very revealing to look with the eyes of the spirit at those souls who in their earthly life were imbued through and through with high ideals, with ideals born from the fire and light of their hearts.

A man who has passed through the gate of death has before him the well-known life-tableau, the memory-picture of his past Earth-life, and interwoven with it is the world of ideals. This world of ideals can come before a man after death in such a way that his feelings concerning it might be expressed as follows: "These ideals, which have fired and illumined my inmost heart, have been my dearest, most intimate treasure, they now wear a strange, unfamiliar aspect. They look as though they did not rightly belong to all that I remember as actual Earth-experience on the physical plane." Yet the dead man feels himself magnetically attracted to these ideals of his; he feels as though he were under their spell. But they may also contain an element that gives him a mild shock; he feels that this element may be dangerous, that it may alienate him from the Earth-evolution, and from what is connected with Earth-evolution in the life between death and a new birth.

In order to express myself quite clearly, I should like to connect what I have said with concrete events. To some of those sitting here they will be known already, but this evening they require to be specially illumined from a certain aspect, that they may be brought into connection with what I have said concerning the nature of human souls. Of recent years, a man of poetic nature joined us. Coming from a life that was dedicated to the purest idealism and had already undergone a mystical deepening, this man joined our Anthroposophical Movement. Although his soul dwelt in a failing body, he devoted himself heart and soul to our spiritual Movement. In the spring of this year we lost him from Earth-life; he passed through the gate of death. He left to mankind a series of wonderful poems, published in a volume that came out shortly after his death.

Owing to the difficulties of his bodily life he was separated in space from our Movement for long periods, either in a lonely spot in the Swiss mountains, or in some other place recommended for his health. But he remained attached to our Movement, from however far away, and his poems, which in certain anthroposophical circles have lately been recited over and over again, are the poetic reflection, as it were, of what we have been developing in Anthroposophy for more than ten years.

Now he has passed through the gate of death, and something very remarkable comes from occult observation of this soul. The significance of the soul's life in that ailing body has become apparent only since death. While working faithfully with us for the progress of our Movement, this soul absorbed something that developed very great strength below the surface of the gradually dying body. This strength was concealed by the ailing body as long as the soul dwelt within it; but now, when one comes into the presence of this soul after death, there shines forth, as it can shine forth only in the spiritual life, the content of the life which this soul absorbed. The cloud-like sphere in which our friend now lives, after having passed through the gate of death, presents itself as a mighty cosmic tableau. For the occult observer this is a most striking sight.

It might perhaps be said that the occult seer is able to cast his gaze round the whole wide sphere of the cosmic world. But it is one thing to allow the gaze to wander round the whole sphere of the cosmic world, and quite another to see, separated out from a particular human soul, something that has the appearance of a mighty tableau, like a painting of what would otherwise be there on its own account in the spiritual world. Just as we have the physical world around us, and then see it reflected in the magnificent paintings of a Raphael or a Michelangelo, so is it in the spiritual world in the case we are speaking of. Just as one never says in the presence of a picture by Michelangelo or Raphael, "Oh, this picture has nothing to give me, for I have all the real world to look at"—so, in observing the tableau that mirrors in a soul what can otherwise be seen in contemplating spiritual reality, one does not say that this soul tableau is not an endless enrichment. And it may be said that there is infinitely more to be learnt in the presence of this friend, who after death contains in his soul a reflection of all we have described from out of the spiritual world in the course of many years, than from direct contemplation of the vastness of spiritual reality.

This is an occult fact. I have repeatedly mentioned it to our friends in other places, and I have now taken from it elements that will be important for our considerations to-day. And this occult fact, as it presents itself in Christian Morgenstern, shows me something else. Anyone who sees how much opposition there still is to the promulgation of occult teaching, as we give it, will often ask questions—I will not call it doubt, but the questions are asked: "What progress will this occult teaching make in human hearts and souls?", and "Is there any guarantee, any assurance, that the work of the Anthroposophical Society will have a continuing influence on the course of the spiritual evolution of humanity?" The sight of what the soul of our friend has become is one such assurance from the occult world. Why? Our friend, who has left behind him the poems, *Wir fanden einen Pfad* ("We found a Path''), lives in the immense cosmic tableau that is like a kind of soul-body for him after death; but while he was connected with us he absorbed into his being our teaching about the Christ. He absorbed this anthroposophical teaching, binding it to his soul until it became the very spiritual heart-blood of his soul; he received it in such a way that for him it was enfilled with the substance of the Christ. The Christ Being flowed into him in the teaching. The Christ, as He lives in our Movement, passed over likewise into his soul.

In contemplating this occult fact, the following presents itself. The man who goes through the gate of death can indeed live in a cosmic tableau of this kind; he will go forward with it through the life that lies between death and a new birth. It will work and be embodied in his whole being, or rather it will ''ensoul'' his whole being, and it will permeate his new Earth-life when he again descends to a life on Earth. Moreover, such a soul receives a germ of perfection for its own life, and progresses in the evolution of the Earth's existence.

All this comes to pass because such a soul has absorbed the teaching into his being. But this particular soul accepted all the teaching, steeped through and spiritualised by the Christ-Being, by the conception of the Christ-Being that we can make our own. All that such a soul absorbed, however, is not merely a treasure stimulating the further evolution of this single soul, but through Christ, who is there for everyone, it works back again upon all mankind. And that cosmic tableau which for clairvoyant eyes is being developed in the soul of him who this spring passed through the gate of death—that Christ-enfilled soul-tableau is for me an assurance that what may be spoken to-day from out of the spiritual worlds will, through the love of Christ, radiate into souls who will come later. They will be set on fire, inspired by it. Not alone will our friend carry forward the Christ-enfilled anthroposophical teaching for his own greater perfecting, but because it has become part of his being it will become an impulse from the spiritual world to the souls who will live in the coming centuries; into them will pour the rays of that which is Christ-enfilled. Your souls cannot take in for themselves alone the Christ-filled spiritual science which is their most precious possession, but they will bear it through epochs of civilisation yet to come. If you enfill this teaching with Christ, it will stream forth as a seed into the whole of humanity because the Christ Being belongs to all mankind. Where Christ is, the treasures of life are not isolated; their fruitfulness for individuals is always there, but at the same time they become a treasure for all mankind.

We must place this clearly before our souls. We see then what a significant difference there is between wisdom that is not filled with Christ and wisdom that is illuminated by the light of Christ. When we come together in a narrower circle of our Society, we are not there for the sake of abstract considerations, but in order to cultivate true occultism, undismayed by what the modern world has to say against it. Hence we are able to touch on matters which can come to our knowledge only through investigation in the spiritual.

A second example calls for mention. In recent years we have had occasion in Munich to perform what we call the Mystery Plays, and Swedish friends have often been present. The performances of these Mystery Plays had to differ in many respects from other performances. There had to be a sense of responsibility to the spiritual world. One could not attend these Mystery Plays as if one were going to an ordinary theatre. Certainly, whatever is accomplished in such a case must proceed from one's own soul-powers. But let us understand clearly that when in our physical life we want to carry out something through the will of our souls, we have to use our muscular power, which is imparted to us from outside and yet belongs to us. If we lack this muscular power, which comes to us from outside, there are some things we cannot do. In a certain sense muscular force belongs to us and yet again not to us. So it is with our spiritual faculties, but our physical forces, our muscular powers, are of no help to us if these faculties are to be active in the spiritual spheres. The powers of the spiritual world itself must come to our aid; the powers and forces which stream out of the spiritual world into our physical world must irradiate and permeate us. It is true that other enterprises somewhat similar in character to our Munich Mystery Plays may be based on a different consciousness, but it was always clear to me that our project could be carried through only in the course of years, that the various impulses might be used only when definite spiritual forces, moving in this direction, flowed into our human forces; when spiritual "Guardian Angel" forces flowed into our human forces.

At the beginning of our spiritual-scientific work, when our very small circle came together at the beginning of this century, it was always easy to count the number present. For a short time a faithful soul was always among them, a soul who through her Karma possessed a special talent for beauty and art.* Even though it was for a short time, the bearer of this soul worked with us, especially in connection with the more intimate spiritual-scientific work that needed to be done at that time. With an inner depth of feeling and an enlightened enthusiasm she worked among us, and absorbed particularly certain cosmological teachings which it was possible to give at that time. And I still remember to-day how at that

* Maria Spettini, actress at the German Imperial Theatre in St. Petersburg.

time a fact came before my soul which may perhaps seem unimportant, but may be mentioned here.

When our Movement began, a periodical which, for well-considered reasons, was called *Lucifer*, came into being. At that time I wrote an article under the title of "Lucifer" which was meant to indicate, in tendency at any rate, the direction in which we wished to work. This article, even if it did not say so in words, laid down the lines which our Anthroposophical Society should follow, and I may say: that article, too, is Christ enfilled. The life-blood of Christianity can flow into those souls who absorb what is in that article. I may now perhaps remark that at the time this article met with the most violent opposition in the circle of the few who had joined us from the old Theosophical Movement. By all of them this article was considered entirely "untheosophical". The personality of whom I have been speaking entered into this article with the warmest possible heart and the deepest inner feeling, and I was able to say to myself: When it is a question of the actual truth, her agreement is of more importance for the progress of the Movement than all the opposition put together. In short, this soul was deeply interwoven with all that was to flow into our spiritual stream.

She soon died; in 1904 she passed through the gate of death. For a while after death she had to struggle through in the spiritual world to find her real identity. Not as early as 1907, but from the time of our Mystery Plays in Munich, from 1909 onwards, and then to an increasing degree as time went on, this soul was always there, guarding and clarifying what I was able to undertake in connection with the Munich Festival Plays. All that this soul, owing to her talent for the beautiful, was able to give to the artistic realisation of our spiritual ideals, worked down out of the spiritual world, as though from the Guardian Angel of our Mystery Plays, in such a way that one felt in oneself the power to take the necessary initiative. Just as in the physical world our muscular energy supports us, so the spiritual force streaming down from the spiritual worlds flowed into one's own spiritual force.

Thus do the dead work with us, so are they present with us. This was yet another case—and here comes the point I must specially speak about to-day—this was again a case in which all that the personality had absorbed in the field of Anthroposophy was not used only to assist her own progress, for it clearly flowed back to us again in something that we ventured to do for the whole Movement. Two possibilities existed. This personality had taken in all that she could, she had it in her soul, and so she could apply it for the sake of her further progress through life and also through the life after death. That is right—it ought to happen so—for if the human soul is to attain its divine goal, it must become ever more and more perfect; it must do all it can to help forward this perfecting. But because this soul had taken into herself the whole purport of what it is to be "Christ-enfilled", what she had absorbed was able not merely to work for herself but to flow down to us—and to become an effective kind of common possession for us all.

That is what Christ brings about when He permeates the fruits of our knowledge. He does not take away all that these fruits of knowledge represent for an individual, but the Christ died for all souls, and when we rise up to that knowledge which must be possessed by all true Earth-men, "Not I, but Christ in me"—when we realise the Christ within us in all that we know, and when we attribute to Christ the forces which we ourselves employ, then all we take into our being works not for ourselves alone, but for the whole of humanity. It becomes fruitful for the whole of humanity. Look at the souls of men all over the Earth. Christ died for them all, and that which you receive in His Name you receive for your own perfecting, but also as a most precious possession that is effective for all mankind.

And now let us return to our introductory words this evening. It was said that when, after death, we look back upon our life-tableau, on all that we have lived through, it appears to us as though our ideals might have something strange about them. We feel in regard to our ideals that they really do not bear us forward to the common life of men, that they have no inherent guarantee of reality in the general life of men; they carry us away from it. Lucifer has a powerful influence over our ideals because they flow in such beauty out of the human soul, but only out of the human soul, and are not rooted in external reality. This is why Lucifer has such power, and it is really the magnetic impulse of Lucifer which we experience in our ideals after death. Lucifer approaches us, and the ideals we have are specially valuable to him, because by the indirect path of these ideals he can draw us to himself. But when we permeate with Christ all that we attain spiritually, when we feel the Christ in us, knowing that what we receive is also received by the Christ in us—''Not I, but Christ in me''—then, when we pass through the gate of death we do not look back upon our ideals as though they tended to alienate us from the world. Our ideals have been committed to Christ and we know that it is Christ who makes our ideals His own concern. He takes our ideals upon Himself. And the individual can say: ''Not I alone can take my ideals upon myself so that they are seeds for humanity on Earth, as surely as the plant-seeds of the present summer are seeds for the

36

earthly plant-robe of the summer to come, but the Christ in me can do this; the Christ in me permeates my ideals with the reality of substance.'' And of those ideals we can say: ''Yes, as men we give expression to ideals on Earth, but in us lives the Christ and He takes them upon Himself.'' These ideals are true seeds of future reality. Christ-enfilled idealism is permeated with the seed of reality, and he who truly understands Christ looks upon ideals in this way. He says: Ideals have not yet in themselves that guarantee of their own reality, their own actuality, which inheres in the plant-seeds for the coming year; but when our ideals are committed to the Christ within us, they are real seeds. Whoever has a true Christ-consciousness and makes his life-substance St. Paul's words: ''Not I, but Christ in me—He is the bearer of my ideals'', he has this realisation. He says: ''There are the ripe, germinating seeds, there are the streams and seas, the hills and valleys—but close by is the world of idealism; this world of idealism is taken over by Christ, and then it is like the seeds of the future world in the world of the present, for the Christ bears our ideals on into the future world as the God of Nature bears the plant-seeds of this year on into the coming year.''

This gives reality to idealism; it removes from the soul those bitter, gloomy doubts which can arise from the feeling: What becomes of the world of ideals that are inwardly bound up with external reality, and with all that I most value? He who takes the Christ Impulse into himself perceives that everything which ripens in the human soul as idealism, as wisdom-treasure, is permeated, saturated through and through with reality. And I have brought the two examples before you in order to show you, out of the occult world, how different is the working of that which is entrusted, Christ-enfilled, to the soul, from that which is entrusted to it only as wisdom which is not Christ-enfilled. What the soul has permeated with Christ in this Earth-life flows down to us quite differently from that which is not Christ-enfilled.

A terrible impression is received when with clairvoyant consciousness one looks out into the spiritual world and sees souls, in whom full Christ-consciousness has not arisen during their last incarnation, fighting for their ideals—fighting for what is dearest to them, because in their ideals Lucifer has power over them which enables him to separate them from the fruits, the real fruits, which the whole world ought to enjoy.

Quite different is the aspect of those who have allowed their soul-wealth, their wisdom-wealth, to become Christ-enfilled. These souls work down into our bodies in this life; they kindle warmth and vitality in our souls. Permeation with the Christ Impulse can be felt as most precious inner soul-warmth, as comfort in the most difficult circumstances, as support in the worst abysses of life. And why? Because he who is truly permeated with the Christ Impulse feels that in whatever conquests his soul achieves, however imperfect they may appear in earthly life, there lies this Christ Impulse as the assurance and guarantee of fulfilment for them. That is why Christ is such a consolation in the doubts of life, such a support for the soul. How much for the souls on Earth remains unfulfilled in life! How much seems to them precious, although in relation to the outer physical world they cannot but regard it as resembling vain hopes of spring. But anything we honestly feel in our soul, anything we can unite with our soul as a valued possession—all this we can commit to Christ; and whatever may be its prospects of realisation, when we have committed it to Christ He bears it forth upon His wings into reality. It is not always necessary to have knowledge of this, but the soul that feels the Christ within it, as the body feels its life-giving blood, feels the warmth, the promise of realisation in this Christ Impulse in respect of all that cannot be realised in the external world, although the soul, with perfect justification, longs for it to be realised.

The fact that clairvoyant consciousness sees these things when it surveys souls after death is a proof of how justifiable is the feeling of the human soul when in all that a man does, in all that he thinks, he feels himself Christ-enfilled, takes the Christ into his soul as comfort, as support, saying in Earth-life: "Not I, but Christ in me!" For a man may indeed say that in this Earth-life! Recall a passage at the beginning of my book, *Theosophy*,* which is meant to indicate one of these points where, at a certain stage of the spiritual life, there is a realisation, of what fills the soul in this earthly life. In a certain place in this book I have drawn attention to the fact that *Tat twam asi*, "Thou art that", upon which the Eastern sages meditate, comes before man as a reality at that moment when the transition from the so-called soul-world into the spiritual world takes place. Look up the passage in question.

But something else can become a reality, in a way that is of immense human significance in relation to St. Paul's words, "Not I, but Christ in me", which the Christ-enfilled soul may say in this life. If a man knows how to experience as inner truth this "Not I, but Christ in me", it comes to powerful fulfilment after death. For what we receive through the words "Not I, but Christ in me", becomes our endowment, our inner nature between death and a new birth, to such an extent that we may impart it as fruit to the whole of humanity. What we so take that we receive it under the

* *Theosophy, An Introduction to the Supersensible Knowledge of The World and the Destination of Man*, Fourth Edition, 1973, Rudolf Steiner Press, London.

aspect of "Not I", Christ makes into a common possession for all humanity. What I receive under the aspect of "Not I", of this I may dare, after death, to say and feel, "Not for me alone, but for all my human brethren!" And then only may I say the words: "Yes, I have loved Him above all, even above myself", and therefore I have hearkened to the command, "Love thy God above all". "Not I, but Christ in me".

And I have fulfilled that other commandment, "Love thy neighbour as thyself", for whatever I have attained for myself will become through the fact that Christ carries it into reality, the common property of all mankind.

We must allow such things as these to work upon us, and then we experience what Christ has to signify in the human soul—how Christ can be the bearer and supporter, the comforter and illuminator of the soul of man. And so we gradually come to enter through our feelings into that which may be called the relation of Christ to the human soul.

LECTURE 3

One of the concepts which must occur to us when we speak of the relation of Christ to the human soul is undoubtedly that of sin and guilt. We know what an incisive significance it had in the Christianity of St. Paul. Our present age, however, is not well adapted for gaining a really deep inner understanding of the wider connections between the concepts "death and sin" and "death and immortality" which are to be found in Paul's writings. That cannot be expected in our materialistic times. Let us recall what I said in the first lecture of this course, that there can be no true immortality of the human soul without a continuation of consciousness after death. An ending of consciousness with death would be equivalent to the fact, which would then have to be accepted, that man is not immortal. An unconscious continuance of man's being after death would mean that the most important part of him, that which makes him a man, would not exist after death. An unconscious human soul surviving after death would not mean much more than the sum of atoms which, as materialism recognises, remain even when the human body is destroyed.

For Paul it was an unshakable conviction that it is possible to speak of immortality only if individual consciousness is maintained. And since he had to regard the individual consciousness as subject to sin and guilt, he would naturally think: If a man's consciousness is obscured or disturbed after death by sin and guilt, or by their results, this signifies that sin and guilt really kill man—they kill him as soul, as spirit. The materialistic consciousness of our time of course is remote from that. Many modern philosophical thinkers are content to speak of a continuance of the life of the human soul, whereas the immortality of man can be identified only with a continuing *conscious* existence of the human soul after death.

Here, certainly, a difficulty may easily arise, especially for the anthroposophical world-view. To approach this difficulty we need only look at the opposition between the concept of guilt and sin and the concept of Karma. Many anthroposophists get over this simply by saying: "We believe in Karma, meaning here a debt which a man contracts in any one of his incarnations; he bears this debt with him, as part of his Karma, and discharges it later; so, in the course of incarnations, a compensation is brought about." Here the difficulty begins. These people then easily say: "How can this be reconciled with the Christian acceptance of the forgiveness of sins through Christ?" And yet the idea of the forgiveness of sins is intimately bound up with true Christianity. We need think of one example: Christ on the Cross between the two malefactors. The malefactor on the left hand mocks at Christ: "If thou wilt be God, help thyself and us!" The malefactor on the right says that the other ought not to speak thus, for both had merited their fate of crucifixion, the just award of their deeds; whereas He was innocent and yet had to experience the same fate. And the malefactor on the right went on to say: "Think of me when thou art in thy kingdom." And Christ answered him: "Verily I say unto thee, to-day thou shalt be with me in Paradise."

It is not permissible merely to gainsay these words or to omit them from the Gospel, for they are very significant.

The difficulty for anthroposophists arises from the question: If this malefactor on the right has to wash away the Karma he has incurred, what does it mean when Christ, as though pardoning and forgiving him, says: "Today thou shalt be with me in Paradise"? An objector may say that the malefactor on the right will have to wash away his Karmic debt, even as the one on the left. Why is a difference made by Christ between the malefactor on the right and the one on the left? There is no doubt at all that here the anthroposophical conception of Karma meets a difficulty that is not easy to solve. It can be solved, however, when we try to probe more deeply into Christianity by means of spiritual science. And now I shall approach the subject from quite another side, a side already known to you, but it can bring certain remarkable circumstances to light.

You know how often we speak of Lucifer and Ahriman, and how Lucifer and Ahriman are represented in my Mystery Plays. If one begins to consider the matter in a human-anthropomorphic sense and simply makes of Lucifer a kind of inner and Ahriman a kind of outer criminal, there will be difficulty in getting on; for we must not forget that Lucifer, besides being the bringer of evil into the world, the inner evil that arises through the passions, is also the bringer of freedom. Lucifer plays an important rôle in the universe, and so does Ahriman.

When we began to speak more of Lucifer and Ahriman, our experience was that many of those associated with us became uneasy; they still had a feeling of what people have always thought of Lucifer—that he is a fearful criminal in the world, against whom one must defend oneself. Naturally, an anthroposophist cannot go all the way with this feeling, for he has to assign to Lucifer an important rôle in the

43

universe—and yet again Lucifer must be regarded as an opponent of the progressive gods, as an enemy who crosses the creative plan of those gods to whom reverence is rightly due. Thus, when we speak of Lucifer in this way, we are ascribing an important role in the universe to an enemy of the gods. And we must do the same for Ahriman.

From this point of view it is easy to understand the human feeling that leads a person to ask: "What is the right attitude to adopt towards Lucifer and Ahriman; am I to love them or to hate them? I really don't know what to do about them." How does all this come about? It should be quite clear from the way in which one speaks of Lucifer and Ahriman that they are Beings who by their whole nature do not belong to the physical plane but have their mission and task in the Cosmos outside the physical plane, in the spiritual worlds. In the lectures given in Munich in the summer of 1913* I laid particular emphasis on the fact that the progressive gods have assigned to Lucifer and Ahriman rôles in the spiritual world; and that discrepancy and disharmony appear only when they bring down their activities into the physical plane and arrogate to themselves rights which are not allotted to them. But we must submit to one fact which the human soul does not readily accept when these matters are under consideration, and it is this: our human judgment holds good only for the physical plane, and—right as it may be for the physical plane—it cannot be simply transferred to the higher worlds. We must therefore gradually accustom ourselves in Anthroposophy to widen our judgments and our

---

* Eight lectures, Munich (24th–31st August, 1913) entitled, *The Secrets of the Threshold*, publ. Rudolf Steiner Press, London.

world of concepts and ideas. It is because materialistically minded men of the present day do not want to widen their judgment, but prefer to keep to judgments which hold good for the physical plane, that they have such difficulty in understanding Anthroposophy, although it is all perfectly intelligible.

If we say, "one power is hostile to another", then on the physical plane it is quite right to say, "enmity is improper, it ought not to exist". But the same thing does not hold good for the higher planes. There, judgment must be widened. Just as in the realm of electricity positive and negative electricity are necessary, so is spiritual hostility necessary in order that the universe may exist in its entirety; it is necessary that the spirits should oppose one another. Here is the truth in the saying of Heraclitos, that strife as well as love constitutes the universe. It is only when Lucifer works upon the human soul, and when through the human soul strife is brought into the physical world, that strife is wrong. But this does not hold good for the higher worlds; there, the hostility of the spirits is an element that belongs to the whole structure, the whole evolution, of the universe. This implies that as soon as we come into the higher worlds we must adopt other standards, other colourings for our judgments. That is why there is often a feeling of shock when we speak of Lucifer and Ahriman on the one hand as the opponents of the gods, and on the other hand as being necessary for the whole course of the cosmic order. Hence we must, above all things, hold firmly in our minds that a man comes into collision with the cosmic order if he allows a judgment which holds good for the physical plane to hold good for the higher worlds also.

Now the root of the whole matter, which must again and

again be emphasised, is that the Christ, as Christ, does not belong with the other beings of the physical plane. From the moment of the Baptism in the Jordan, a Being who had not previously existed on Earth, a Being who does not belong to the order of Earth-beings, entered into the corporeality of Jesus of Nazareth. Thus in Christ we are concerned with a Being who could truly say to the disciples: "I am from above, but ye are from below", which means: "I am a Being of the kingdom of Heaven, ye are of the kingdom of Earth."

Now let us consider the consequences of this. Must an earthly judgment that is entirely justifiable as such, and that everyone on Earth must maintain, be also the judgment of that Cosmic Being who, as Christ, entered the Jesus body? That Being who passed into the body of Jesus at the Baptism in the Jordan applies not an earthly but a heavenly judgment. He must judge differently from men.

And now let us consider the whole import of the words spoken on Golgotha. The malefactor on the left believes that in the Christ merely an earthly being is present, not a Being whose realm is beyond the earthly kingdom. But just before death there comes to the consciousness of the malefactor on the right: "Thy kingdom, O Christ, is another; think of me when thou art in Thy kingdom." At this moment the malefactor on the right shows that he has a dim idea of the fact that Christ belongs to another kingdom, where a power of judgment quite different from that obtaining on the Earth holds sway. Then, out of the consciousness that He stands in His kingdom, Christ can answer: "Verily, because thou hast some dim foreboding of my kingdom, this day (that is, with death) thou shalt be with me in my kingdom." This indicates the super-earthly Christ power that draws up the

46

human individuality into a spiritual kingdom. Earthly judgment, human judgment, must of course say: "As regards his Karma, the right-hand malefactor will have to make compensation for his guilt, even as the one on the left." For heavenly judgment, however, something else holds good. But that is only the beginning of the matter, for of course it might now be said: "Yes, then the judgment of Heaven contradicts that of the Earth. How can Christ forgive where earthly judgment demands karmic justice?"

This is indeed a difficult question, but we will try to approach it more closely in the course of this lecture. I lay special emphasis on the fact that we are touching here on one of the most difficult questions of occult science. We must make a distinction which the human soul does not willingly make, because it does not like following out the matter to its ultimate consequences, and there are indeed some difficulties in so doing. We shall find it, as I have said, a difficult subject, and you will perhaps have to turn the question over in your minds many times in order to get at its real essence.

To start with, we must make a distinction. We must first consider how, through Karma, objective justice is fulfilled. Here we must clearly understand that a man is certainly subject to his Karma; he has to make karmic compensation for unjust deeds, and if we think more deeply about it, we can see that he will not really wish it otherwise. For suppose a man has done another person wrong; in the moment of doing so he is further from fulfilment than he was before, and he can recover the lost ground only by making compensation for his unjust act. He must wish to make compensation, for only by so doing can he bring himself back to the stage he had reached before committing the act. Thus for the

47

sake of our own progress we are bound to wish that Karma should be there as objective justice. When we grasp the true meaning of human freedom, we can have no wish that a sin should be so forgiven us that we would no longer need to pay it off in our Karma. For example, a man who puts out the eyes of another is more imperfect than one who does not, and in his later Karma it must come to pass that he does a correspondingly good deed, for only then will he be inwardly again the man he was before he committed the sin. So if we rightly consider the nature of man, we cannot suppose that when a man has put out the eyes of another it will be forgiven him, and that Karma will be in some way adjusted. Hence there is rightness in the fact that we are not excused a farthing of our Karma, but must pay our debts in full.

But something else comes in. The guilt, the sins, with which we are laden are not merely our own affair; they are an objective cosmic fact which means something for the universe also. That is where the distinction must be made. The crimes we have committed are compensated through our Karma, but the act of putting out another person's eyes is an accomplished fact. If we have, let us say, put out someone's eyes in a present incarnation, and then in the next incarnation we do something that makes compensation for this act, yet for the objective course of the universe the fact will remain that so many hundred years ago we put out someone's eyes. That is an objective fact in the universe. As far as we are concerned, we make compensation for it later. The stain that we have personally contracted is adjusted in our Karma, but the objective fact remains—we cannot efface that by removing our own imperfection. We must discriminate between the consequences of a sin for ourselves, and the consequences of a sin for the objective course of the world. It is highly important that we should make this distinction. And I may now perhaps introduce an occult observation that will make the matter clearer.

If one surveys the course of human evolution since the Mystery of Golgotha and approaches the Akashic Record without being permeated with the Christ Being, it is easy, very easy indeed, to be led into error, for one will find records which very often do not coincide with the karmic evolution of the individuals concerned. For example, let us suppose that in, say, the year 733 some man lived and incurred heavy guilt. The person now examining the Akashic Record may at first have no connection with the Christ Being. And behold—the man's guilt cannot be found in the Akashic Record. Examination of the Karma of this man in a later incarnation reveals that there is something still in his Karma which he has to wipe out. That must have existed in the Akashic Record at a certain point of time, but it is no longer there. A strange contradiction! This is an objective fact which may occur in any cases. I may meet a man today, and if through grace I am permitted to know something about his Karma, I may perhaps find that some misfortune or stroke of fate that has fallen on him stands in his Karma, that it is an adjustment of earlier guilt. If I turn to his earlier incarnations and examine what he did then, I do not find his guilty deed registered in the Akashic Record. How does this come about?

The reason is that Christ has taken upon Himself the objective debt. In the moment that I permeate myself with Christ, I discover the deed when I examine the Akashic Record. Christ has taken it into His kingdom and He bears it further, so that when I look away from Christ I cannot find it in the Akashic Record. This distinction must be kept clearly in mind: karmic justice remains, but Christ intervenes in the effects of the guilt in the spiritual world. He takes over the debt into His kingdom and bears it further. Christ is that Being who, because He is of another kingdom, is able to blot out in the world our debts and our sins, taking them upon Himself.

What is it that Christ on the Cross of Golgotha really conveys to the malefactor on the left? He does not utter it, but in the fact that He does not utter it lies its essence, He says to the malefactor on the left: What thou has done will continue to work in the spiritual world, and not merely in the physical world. To the malefactor on the right He says: "Today thou shalt be with me in Paradise." This means: "I am beside thine act; through thy Karma thou wilt have later on to do for thyself all that the act signifies for thee, but what the act signifies for the universe, that"—if I may use a trivial expression—"is my concern." This is what Christ says. The distinction made here is certainly an important one, and significant not only for the time after the Mystery of Golgotha, but also for the time before the Mystery of Golgotha.

Some of our friends will remember that in earlier lectures I have called attention to the fact that Christ really did descend to the dead after His death; this- is not a mere legend. He thereby accomplished something also for the souls who in previous ages had laden themselves with guilt and sins. Error now comes in if a man, without being permeated with Christ, investigates in the Akashic Record the time before the Mystery of Golgotha. He will continually make errors in his reading of the Akashic Record. Hence, for example, I was not at all surprised that Leadbeater, who in reality knows nothing about Christ, should have made the most abstruse statements concerning the evolution of the Earth in his book, *Man: How, Whence and Whither*. For only through permeation with the Christ Impulse is the soul capable of really seeing things as they are, and how they have been regulated in the evolution of the Earth on the basis of the Mystery of Golgotha, though they occurred before it.

Karma is an affair of the successive incarnations of man. The significance of karmic justice must be looked at with our earthly judgment. That which Christ does for humanity must be measured by a judgment that belongs to worlds other than this Earth-world. And suppose that were not so? Let us think of the end of the Earth, of the time when men will have passed through their earthly incarnations. Most certainly it will come to pass that all debts will have to be paid to the last farthing. Human souls will have had to balance their Karma in a certain way. But let us imagine that all guilt had continued to exist in the Earth-world, that all guilt would go on working there. Then at the end of the Earth period human beings would be there with their Karma balanced, but the Earth would not be ready to develop into the Jupiter condition; the whole of Earth humanity would be there without a dwelling-place, without the possibility of developing onwards to Jupiter. The fact that the whole Earth develops along with man is a result of the deed of Christ. All the guilt and debt that would otherwise have piled up would cast the Earth into darkness and we should have no planet for our further evolution. In our Karma we can take care of ourselves, but not of humanity as a whole, and not of that which in Earth-evolution is connected with the whole evolution of humanity.

So let us realise that Karma will not be taken from us, but that our debts and sins will be wiped out from the Earth-evolution through what has come in with the Mystery of Golgotha. Now we must, of course, realise clearly that all this cannot be bestowed on man without his co-operation—it cannot be his unless he does something. And that is clearly brought before us in the utterance from the Cross of Golgotha which I have quoted. It is very definitely shown to us how the soul of the malefactor on the right received a dim idea of a supersensible kingdom wherein things proceed otherwise than in the mere earthly kingdom. Man must fill his soul with the substance of the Christ Being; he must, as it were, have taken something of the Christ into his soul, so that Christ is active in him and bears him into a kingdom where man has indeed no power to make his Karma ineffective, but where it comes to pass through Christ that our debts and sins are blotted out from our external world.

This has been wonderfully represented in painting. There is no-one upon whom a picture such as "Christ as Judge at the Last Judgment", by Michelangelo in the Sistine Chapel, can fail to make a deep impression. What really underlies such a picture? Let us take, not the deep esoteric fact, but the picture that is here presented to our souls. We see the righteous and the sinners. It would have been possible to present this picture differently from the way in which Michelangelo, as a Christian, has painted it. There was the possibility that at the end of the Earth, men, seeing their Karma, might have said to themselves: "Yes, I have indeed wiped off my Karma, but everywhere in the spiritual, written on tablets of brass, are my guilt and my sins, and they weigh heavily on the Earth; they will destroy the Earth. As far as I am concerned I have made compensation, but there the guilt stands, every-where." That would not, however, be the truth; it could have been shown, but it would not be the truth. For through the fact of Christ's death upon Golgotha, men will not see the tablets of their guilt and sin, but they will see Him who has taken them upon himself; they will see, united with the Being of Christ, all that would otherwise be spread out in the Akashic Record. In place of the Akashic Record, the Christ stands before them, having taken all upon Himself.

We are looking into deep secrets of the Earth's exis-tence. But what is necessary in order to fathom the true state of things in this domain? It is this: that men, no matter whether they are righteous or sinful, should have the possibility of looking upon Christ, that they should not look upon an empty place where the Christ should stand. The connection with Christ is necessary, and the malefactor on the right shows us his connection with Christ by what he says. And although the Christ has given to those who work in His spirit the behest to forgive sins, this never means encroaching upon Karma. What it does mean is that the earthly kingdom will be rescued for him who stands in relationship to Christ, rescued from the spiritual consequences of guilt and sin, which are objective facts even when a later Karma has made compensation for them.

What does it signify for the human soul when one who may so speak says in the name of Christ: "Thy sins are forgiven thee!" It means that he is able to assert: "Thou hast indeed to await thy karmic settlement; but Christ has transformed thy guilt and sin so that later thou mayest not have the terrible sorrow of looking back upon thy guilt and seeing that through it thou hast destroyed a part of the Earth's existence." Christ blots it out. But a certain consciousness is necessary and those who would forgive sins may rightly demand it—a consciousness of the guilt, and consciousness that Christ has the power to take it upon Himself. For the saying: "Thy sins are forgiven thee", denotes a cosmic fact and not a karmic fact.

Christ shows His relation to this so wonderfully in a certain passage—so wonderfully that it penetrates deep, deep into our hearts. Let us call up in our souls the scene where the woman taken in adultery comes before Him, with those who were condemning her. They bring the woman before Him and in two different ways Christ meets them. He writes in the Earth; and He forgives, He does not judge; He does not condemn. Why does He write in the Earth? Because Karma works, because Karma is objective justice. For the adulteress, her act cannot be obliterated. Christ writes it in the Earth.

But with the spiritual, the not-earthly consequence, it is otherwise. Christ takes upon Himself the spiritual consequence. "He forgives" does not mean that He blots out in the absolute sense, but that He takes upon Himself the consequences of the objective act.

Now let us think of all that it signifies when the human soul is able to say to itself: "Yes, I have done this or that in the world. It does not impair my evolution, for I do not remain as imperfect as I was when I committed the deed; I am permitted to overcome that imperfection in the further course of my Karma by making compensation for the deed. But I cannot undo it for the Earth-evolution." Man would have to bear unspeakable suffering if a Being had not united Himself with the Earth, a Being who undoes for the Earth that which we cannot change. This Being is the Christ. He takes away from

54

us, not subjective Karma, but the objective spiritual effects of the acts, the guilt. That is what we must follow up in our hearts, and then for the first time we shall understand that Christ is in truth that Being who is bound up with the whole of Earth-humanity. For the Earth is there for the sake of mankind, and so Christ is connected also with the whole Earth. It is a weakness of man, as a consequence of the Luciferic temptation, that although he is indeed able to redeem himself subjectively through Karma, he cannot redeem the Earth at the same time. That is accomplished by the Cosmic Being, the Christ.

And now we understand why many anthroposophists cannot realise that Christianity is in full accord with the idea of Karma. They are people who bring into Anthroposophy the most intense egoism, a super-egoism; certainly they do not put it into words, but still they really think and feel: "If I can only redeem myself through my Karma, what does the world matter to me? Let it do what it will!" These anthroposophists are quite satisfied if they can speak of karmic adjustment. But there is a great deal more to be done. Man would be a purely Luciferic being if he were to think only of himself. Man is a member of the whole world, and he must think about it in the sense that he can indeed be egotistically redeemed through his Karma, but is not able to redeem the whole Earth-existence. Here the Christ enters. At the moment when we decide not to think only of our ego, we must think about something other than our ego. Of what must we think? Of the "Christ in me", as Paul says; then indeed we are united with Him in the whole Earth-existence. We do not then think of our self-redemption, but we say: "Not I and my own redemption—not I, but the Christ in me and the redemption of the Earth."

55

Many believe they may call themselves true Christians, and yet they speak of others—anthroposophical Christians, for instance—as heretics. There is very little true Christian feeling here. The question may perhaps be permitted: "Is it really Christian to think that I may do whatever I like and that Christ came into the world in order to take it all away from me and to forgive my sins, so that I need have nothing more to do with my Karma, with my sins?" I think there is another word more applicable to such a way of thinking than the word "Christian"; perhaps the word "convenient" would be better. "Convenient" it would certainly be if a man had only to repent, and then all the sins he had committed in the world were obliterated from the whole of his later Karma. The sin is not blotted out from Karma; but it can be blotted out from the Earth-evolution, and this it is that man cannot do because of the human weakness that results from the Luciferic temptation. Christ accomplishes this. With the remission of sins we are saved from the pain of having added an objective debt to the Earth-evolution for all eternity. Only, of course, we must have a serious interest in this. When we have this true understanding of Christ, a greater earnestness will manifest itself in many other ways as well. Many elements will fall away from those conceptions of Christ which may well seem full of triviality and cynicism to the man whose soul has absorbed the Christ-conception in all seriousness. For all that has been said to-day, and it can be proved point by point from the most significant passages of the New Testament, tells us that everything Christ is for us derives from the fact that He is not a Being like other men, but a Being who, from above— that is, from out of the Cosmos—entered into Earth-evolution at the baptism by John in Jordan. Everything speaks for the cosmic nature of Christ. And he who deeply grasps Christ's attitude towards sin and debt may speak thus: "Because man in the course of the Earth's existence could not blot out his guilt for the whole Earth, a Cosmic Being had to descend in order that the Earth's debt might be discharged."

True Christianity must needs regard Christ as a Cosmic Being. It cannot do otherwise. Then, however, our soul will be deeply permeated by what is meant in the words, "Not I, but Christ in me." For then from this knowledge there radiates into our soul something that I can express only in these words: "When I am able to say, 'Not I, but Christ in me', in that moment I acknowledge that I shall be raised from the Earth-sphere, that in me there lives something that has significance for the Cosmos, and that I am counted worthy, as man, to bear a super-earthly element in my soul, just as I bear within me a super-earthly being in all that has entered into me from Saturn, Sun and Moon."

The consciousness of being permeated with Christ will become of immense importance. And with St. Paul's saying, "Not I, but Christ in me", a man will connect the feeling that his inner responsibility to Christ must be taken in deep, deep earnestness. Anthroposophy will bring into the Christ-consciousness this feeling of responsibility in such a way that we shall not presume on every occasion to say: "I thought so, and because I thought so, I had a right to say it." Our materialistic age is carrying this further and further. "I was convinced of this and therefore I had a right to say it." But is it not a profanation of the Christ in us, a fresh crucifixion of the Christ in us, that at any moment when we believe something or other, we cry it out to the world, or send it out into the world in writing, without having investigated it?

When the full significance of Christ comes home to mankind, the individual will feel that he must be more and more conscientious, must prove himself worthy of Christ, this Cosmic Principle, within him.

It may be readily believed that those who do not want to receive Christ as a Cosmic Principle, but are ready at every opportunity to repent an offence, will first tell all kinds of lies about their fellow-men and will then want to wipe out the lies. Anyone who wishes to give worthy proof of the Christ in his soul will first ask himself whether he ought to say a certain thing, even though he may for the moment be convinced of it.

Many things will be changed when a true conception of Christ comes into the world. All those countless people to-day who write, or disfigure paper with printer's ink, because they briskly write down things of which they have no knowledge, will come to realise that by so doing they are putting the Christ in the human soul to shame. And then the excuse will cease: "Well, I thought it was so, I said it in good faith." Christ wants more than "good faith"; Christ would fain lead men to the truth. He Himself has said, "The truth will make you free." But where has Christ ever said that it is possible for anyone who is thinking in *his* sense to shout out or put forth in writing something or other of which he really knows nothing? Much indeed will be changed! A great deal of modern writing will be ruled out when people proceed from the principle of proving themselves worthy of the saying: "Not I, but Christ in me." The cancer of our decadent civilisation will be rooted out when silence falls on those voices which, without real conviction, cry everything out into the world, or cover paper with printer's ink irresponsibly, without being first convinced that they are speaking the truth.

The "Christian conscience", as we may call it in a certain sense, will arise in increasing measure as human souls become more and more conscious of the presence of Christ, and the saying of Paul becomes true: "Not I, but Christ in me!"

More and more will souls be imbued with the consciousness that a man ought not to say merely what he "thinks", but must prove the objective truth of what he says.

Christ will be for the soul a teacher of truth, a teacher of the highest sense of responsibility. In these ways He will permeate souls when they come to experience the whole import of the saying: "Not I, but Christ in me."

LECTURE 4

Mankind is always in need of truths which cannot, in every age, be wholly understood. The assimilation of truths is not significant only for our knowledge; truths themselves contain life-force. By permeating ourselves with truth we permeate our soul-nature with an element drawn from the objective world, just as we must permeate our physical being with air taken from outside in order to live. Deep truths are indeed expressed in great religious revelations, but in such a form that their real inner meaning is often not understood until much, much later.

The New Testament has been written; the New Testament stands there as a record for humanity—but the whole future course of the Earth's evolution will be required for a full understanding of the New Testament to be reached. In the future, men will acquire much knowledge of the external world, and of the spiritual world also; and if taken in the right sense it will all contribute to an understanding of the New Testament. The understanding comes about gradually, but the New Testament is written in a simple form so that it can be absorbed and, later, gradually understood. To permeate ourselves with the truth that resides in the New Testament is not without significance, even if we cannot yet understand the truth in its deepest inwardness. Later on, truth becomes cognitional force, but it is already life-force, in so far as it is imbibed in a more or less childlike form. And if the questions we began to consider yesterday are to be understood in the sense in which they are imparted in the New Testament, we need knowledge of greater depth, greater insight into the spiritual world and its mysteries.

If we are to carry further the studies we began yesterday, we must again examine some occult mysteries, for they will be able to guide us to a further understanding of the riddle of guilt and sin, and from this point of view throw light on the relation of Christ to the human soul.

In the course of our anthroposophical work we have often been faced with a point of view which may be put as a question, a question often asked: Why did Christ die in a human body? Here indeed is a fundamental question concerning the Mystery of Golgotha. Why did Christ die, why did the God die, in a human body?

The God died because the evolution of the universe made it necessary that He should be able to enter into humanity; it was necessary that a God of the upper worlds should become the leader of the Earth-evolution. For this reason Christ had to become related to death. Related to death! One could wish that this expression will come to be deeply understood by the soul of man.

As a rule a man encounters death only when he sees another person die, or in other phenomena akin to death which are to be found in the world, or in the certainty that he must himself pass through the gate of death when his present incarnation is over. But that is only the external aspect of death. Death is present in a quite different form in the world in which we live, and attention must be drawn to this. Let us start from a quite ordinary, everyday phenomenon. We breathe the air in and we breathe it out again; but the air undergoes a change. When the air is exhaled it is dead air; as exhaled air it cannot be inhaled again, for exhaled air is deadly. I indicate this only in order that you may understand the meaning of the occult saying: "When the air enters into men, it dies." The living element in the air does indeed die when it enters into man. That, however, is only *one* phenomenon. The ray of light which penetrates our eye must likewise die, and we should gain nothing from the rays of light if our eye did not set itself up against the ray of light, as our lungs do against the air. The light that enters into our eye dies in our eye; and through the death of the light in our eye it comes about that we see. We are filled with much that has to die in us in order that we may have our Earth-consciousness. Corporeally we kill the air; we kill also the rays of light which penetrate us, and so we kill in many ways.

When we call spiritual science to our aid, we distinguish four grades of substance—earth, water, air and warmth. We then enter the realm where we speak of warmth-ether, of light-ether. As far up as the light-ether we kill that which penetrates us; we slay it unceasingly in order that we may have our Earth-consciousness. But there is something we cannot kill by our Earth-existence. We know that above the light-ether there is the so-called chemical ether, and then there comes the life-ether. These are the two kinds of ether that we cannot kill. But because of this, they have no special participation in us. If we were able to kill the chemical ether, the waves of the Harmony of the Spheres would sound perpetually into our physical body, and we should perpetually destroy these waves with our physical life. And if we could also kill the life-ether, we should destroy and continuously kill within ourselves the cosmic life that streams down to the Earth. In earthly sound we are given a substitute, but it is not to be compared with what we should hear if the chemical ether were audible to us as physical human beings. For physical sound is a product of the air and is not the spiritual sound; it is only a substitute for the spiritual sound.

When the Luciferic temptation came, the progressive gods were obliged to place man in a sphere where, from the life-ether downwards, death lives in his physical body. But at that time the progressive gods said—and the words are there in the Bible—"Man has come to know the distinction between Good and Evil, but Life he is not to have. Of the Tree of Life he shall not eat." In occultism, we can continue the sentence, "Of the Tree of Life man shall not eat", by adding the words, "and the Spirit of Matter he shall not hear." Of the Tree of Life man shall not eat and the Spirit of Matter he shall not hear! These are the regions which were closed to man. Only through a certain procedure in the old Mysteries were the tones of the Sphere-Music and the Cosmic Life, pulsating through the universe, revealed to those who were to be initiated when it was given them, outside the body, to see the Christ in advance. Hence it is that the old philosophers speak of the Music of the Spheres.

In drawing attention to this, we indicate at the same time those regions from which the Christ came to us at the time of the baptism by John in the Jordan. Whence did Christ come? He came from those regions which had been closed to man as a result of the Luciferic temptation—from the region of the Music of the Spheres and from the region of Cosmic Life. These regions had to be forgotten by man because of the Luciferic temptation at the beginning of Earth-evolution. At the baptism by John in the Jordan, Christ entered into a human body, and that which permeated this human body was the spiritual essence of the Harmony of the Spheres, the spiritual essence of the Cosmic Life—the element that still belonged to the human soul during the first phase of its time on Earth, but from which the human soul had to be shut out as a result of the Luciferic temptation. In this sense also man is related to spirit. With his soul he really belongs to the region of the Music of the Spheres and to the region of the Word, of the living Cosmic Ether. But he was cast out from those regions. They were to be restored to him in order that he might gradually be permeated again by the spiritual elements from which he had been exiled. So it is that from the standpoint of spiritual science the words of St. John's Gospel touch us so deeply: In the primal beginning, when man was not yet subject to temptation, was the Logos. Man belonged to the Logos . . . the Logos was with God, and man was with the Logos, with God. And through the baptism by John in the Jordan the Logos entered into human evolution—He became Man.

Here we have the all-important connection. Let us leave this truth as it stands there, and approach the question from another side. Life as a whole shows itself to us only from the external side. Otherwise man would know all the time how he absorbs the corpse of the light into his eye when he sees.

What was it that the Christ had to undertake in order that the fulfilment of St. Paul's saying, "Not I, but Christ in me", might be made possible? It had to be possible that Christ should permeate the nature of man; but the nature of man is filled with what is slain by human nature in Earth-existence, from the light-ether downwards—the light-ether that dies in the human eye. The nature of man is filled with death; but the life-element in the two highest kinds of ether was withdrawn in order that human nature might not be laden with their death also. In order that Christ might dwell in us, He had therefore to become related to death, related to all the death that is spread out in the world, from the light down to the depths of materiality. Christ had to be able to pass into all that we bear within us as the corpse of the light, of the warmth, of the air, and so on. It was only because He was able to become related to death that He could become related to man. And we must feel in our souls that the God had to die so that he might be able to enfill us, we who had acquired death as a result of the Luciferic temptation, so that we might be able to say: "Christ in us."

Many other things are hidden for man behind sense-existence. He turns his gaze upon the plant-world; he sees how the light of the Sun conjures the plants out of the soil. Science teaches us that light is necessary for the growth of plants, but that is only half the truth. Anyone who looks at the plants with clairvoyant sight sees living spiritual elements rising out of them. The light dips down into the plants and rises again out of them as a living spiritual element; light comes down into the plants in order to be transformed in them and to be born again as a living spiritual element. In the animals it is the chemical ether that enters, and this chemical ether is not perceptible to man; if he could be aware of it, it would sound forth spiritually. The animals transform this ether into water-spirits. The plants transform light into air-spirits; animals transform the spirit active in the chemical ether into water-spirits. Finally, the cosmic ether, or life-ether, which man is prevented from killing and without which he could not live at all—he transforms the life-ether into earth-spirits.

In a course of lectures given in Karlsruhe, "From Jesus to Christ",* I once spoke of the human "phantom". This is not the time for drawing the connecting threads between what is to be said here and what was said then about the human "phantom", but such connecting threads do exist and you

*From Jesus to Christ, ten lectures, Karlsruhe (5th–14th October, 1911), First edition, 1973, Rudolf Steiner Press, London.

will perhaps find them for yourselves. Today I have to present the matter from another side.

There is perpetually engendered in man something that is also spiritual—the *life* in him. This is forever passing out into the world. Man projects an aura around him, an aura of rays whereby he continually enriches the earthly-spiritual element of the Earth. This earthly-spiritual element of the Earth, however, contains all the qualities, moral or otherwise, that man has acquired and bears within himself, for he sends it all out into his earthly environment. This is absolutely true. Clairvoyant sight perceives how man sends out his moral, intellectual and aesthetic aura into the world, and how this aura continues to live as earthly spirit in the spirituality of the Earth. As a comet draws its tail through the Cosmos, so does man draw through the whole of earthly life the spiritual aura which he projects. This spiritual aura is held together, phantom-like, during a man's life, but at the same time it rays out into the world his moral and intellectual properties of soul.

When in our occult studies we go back to the times before the Mystery of Golgotha, we find that the men of those days simply radiated this phantom-like entity, which contained their moral qualities, into the external world, into the external spiritual aura of the Earth. But humanity developed in the course of the Earth's existence, and just at the epoch where the Mystery of Golgotha came to pass, a certain stage had been reached in the evolution of this phantom-like entity. In earlier times it was much more evanescent; by the time of the Mystery of Golgotha it had become denser, had more form; and into this phantom-like entity there was now mingled, as a fundamental characteristic, the death which man develops in himself by killing the ray of light that enters into his eye, and so on, as I have explained. These earth-spirit entities which radiate from man are like a stillborn child, because he imparts his death to them. If Christ had not come upon Earth, then, during the sojourn of their souls in earthly bodies, human beings could have continuously rayed out entities with the impress of death upon them. And with this impress of death there would have been bound up the moral qualities of man of which we spoke yesterday: objective guilt and objective sin. They would have lain within it.

Let us suppose that the Christ had not come. What would have happened in the evolution of the Earth? From the time in which the Mystery of Golgotha would otherwise have taken place, men would have spiritually created dense forms to which they had imparted death. And these dense forms would have become the very things that had to pass over to the Jupiter stage with the Earth. Man would have imparted death to the Earth. A dead Earth would have given birth to a dead Jupiter.

It could not have been otherwise, because if the Mystery of Golgotha had not come about, man would not have been able to permeate the radiations he gives out with the essences of the Music of the Spheres and the Cosmic Life. These essences would not have been there; they would not have flowed into the human radiations; but Christ brought them back through the Mystery of Golgotha. And when there is a fulfilment of the words, "Not I, but Christ in me", when we bring about a relationship to Christ within ourselves, that which rays out from us and would otherwise be dead, is made living. Because we bear death within us, the living Christ has to permeate us, in order that He may give life to the spiritual Earth-being that we leave behind us. Christ, the living Logos, permeates and gives life to the objective guilt and sin which detaches itself from us and is not carried further in our Karma, and because He gives it life, a living Earth will evolve into a living Jupiter. This is the outcome of the Mystery of Golgotha.

The soul, if it reflects, can receive Christ in the following way. It can realise that there was once a time when man was within the bosom of the divine Logos. But man had to succumb to the temptation of Lucifer. He took death into himself. Into him there passed the germ by which he would have brought a dead Earth to birth as a dead Jupiter. The endowment which, before the temptation, the human soul had been destined to receive for its Earth-existence was left behind. With Christ it entered again into man's Earth-existence.

When man takes Christ into himself, so as to feel permeated with Christ, he is able to say to himself: "The endowment which the gods had allocated to me before the Luciferic temptation, but which owing to the temptation by Lucifer had to remain behind in the Cosmos, enters into my soul with the Christ. The soul becomes whole again for the first time by taking the Christ into itself. Only then am I fully soul; only then am I again all that the gods intended me to be from the very beginning of the Earth." "Am I really a soul without Christ?" man asks himself, and he feels that it is through Christ that he first becomes the soul that the guiding divine Beings meant him to be. This is the wonderful feeling of "home" that souls can have with Christ; for out of the primal cosmic home of the soul of man the Christ descended, in order to give back to the soul of man that which had to be lost on Earth as a result of the temptation by Lucifer. The Christ leads the soul up again to its primordial home, the home allotted to it by the gods.

That is the bliss and the blessing in the actual experience of Christ in the human soul. It was this that gave such bliss to certain Christian mystics in the Middle Ages. They may have written much which in itself seems to be too strongly coloured by the senses, but fundamentally it was spiritual. Such Christian mystics as those who joined Bernard of Clairvaux, and others, felt that the human soul was as a bride who had lost her bridegroom at the primal beginning of the Earth; and when Christ entered into their souls, filling them with life and soul and spirit, they experienced Christ as the soul-bridegroom who united Himself with the soul; the bridegroom who had been lost when the soul forsook her original home in order to follow Lucifer along the path of freedom, the path of differentiation between good and evil.

When the soul of man really lives into Christ, feeling that Christ is the living Being who from the death on Golgotha flowed out into the atmosphere of the Earth and can flow into the soul, it feels itself inwardly vivified through the Christ. The soul feels a transition from death into life.

So long as we have to live out our earthly existence in human bodies—and this will continue far into a remote future—we cannot hear directly the Music of the Spheres or have direct experience of the Cosmic Life. But we can experience the incoming of the Christ, and so we can receive, by proxy as it were, that which would otherwise come to us from the Music of the Spheres and the Cosmic Life.

Pythagoras, an Initiate of the ancient Mysteries, spoke of the Music of the Spheres. He had gone through the process whereby the soul passes out of the body, and he could then be carried away into the spiritual worlds. There he saw the Christ who was later to come to the Earth. Since the Mystery of Golgotha we cannot speak of the Music of the Spheres as did Pythagoras, but we can speak of it in another way. An initiate might even today speak as Pythagoras did; but the ordinary inhabitant of the Earth in his physical body can speak of the Music of the Spheres and of the Cosmic Life only when he experiences in his soul, "Not I, but Christ in me", for the Christ within him has lived in the Music of the Spheres and in the Cosmic Life. But we must go through this experience in ourselves; we must really receive the Christ into our souls.

Let us suppose that a man were to fight against this, that he did not wish to receive Christ into his soul. Then he would come to the end of the Earth period, and in the nebulous spirit-structure that had then taken shape out of the Earth-spirits arising in the course of human evolution, he would have all the phantom-like beings which had issued from him in former incarnations. They would all be there. The tendency indicated here would lead to a dead Earth, and this would pass over, dead, to Jupiter. At the end of the Earth period a man might have carried through and completely absolved his Karma; he might have made personal compensation for all his imperfect deeds; he might have become whole in his soul-being, in his ego, but the objective sin and guilt would remain. That is an absolute truth, for we do not live only for ourselves, so that by adjusting our Karma we may become egotistically more nearly perfect; we live for the world, and at the end of the ages the remains of our Earth incarnations will stand there like a mighty tableau if we have not taken into us the living Christ.

When we connect what was said yesterday with what is being said today (and it is really the same, only seen from two sides) we understand how Christ takes upon Himself the guilt and sin of Earth humanity, in so far as these are objective guilt and sin. And if we have inwardly realised this "Not I, but Christ in me", the Christ in us, then He takes over the objective remains of our incarnations, and they stand there vivified by Christ, irradiated by Christ and permeated by His life. Yes, the remains of our incarnations stand there, and what do they come to, taken as a whole?

Because Christ unites them all—Christ who belongs to all mankind in the present and in the future—the remains of the single incarnations are all compressed together. Every human soul lives in successive incarnations. From each incarnation certain relics or remains are left, as we have described. Further incarnations will leave other remains, and so on, up to the end of the Earth period. If these relics are permeated by Christ, they are compressed together. Compress what is rarefied and you will get density. Spirit also becomes dense, and so our collective Earth-incarnations are united into a spiritual body. This body belongs to us; we need it because we evolve onwards to Jupiter, and it will be the starting-point of our embodiment on Jupiter. At the end of the Earth period we shall stand there with the soul—whatever the particular karma of the soul may be—we shall stand there before our earthly relics which have been gathered together by Christ, and we shall have to unite with them in order to pass over with them to Jupiter.

We shall rise again in the body, in the earthly body that has condensed out of the separate incarnations. Truly, my dear friends, from a heart profoundly moved I utter these words: "In the body we shall rise again!"

In these days, young people of sixteen and even less are beginning to claim a creed of their own, and to talk of having happily grown beyond such nonsense as the "Resurrection of the Body". But those who seek to deepen their occult knowledge of the mysteries of the universe strive gradually to rise to an understanding of what has been said to mankind, because—as I explained at the beginning of the lecture—it had first of all to be *said*, in order that men might grasp it as life-truth and come to understand it later. The resurrection of the body is a reality, but our soul must feel that it will rise again with the earthly relics that have been collected, brought together by Christ, by the spiritual body that is permeated with Christ. This is what our soul must learn to understand. For let us suppose that, because of our not having received into ourselves the living Christ, we could not approach this Earth-body, with its sin and guilt, and unite with it. If we had rejected the Christ, the relics of our various incarnations would be scattered at the end of the Earth period; they would have remained, but they would not have been gathered together by the Christ who spiritualises the whole of humanity. We should stand there as souls at the end of the Earth period and we should be bound to the Earth, to that part of the Earth which remains dead in our relics. Certainly our souls would be free in the spirit in an egotistic sense, but we would be unable to approach our bodily relics. Such souls are the booty of Lucifer, for he strives to thwart the true goal of the Earth; he tries to prevent souls from reaching their Earth-goal, to hold them back in the spiritual world. And in the Jupiter period Lucifer will send over what has remained of scattered Earth-relics as a dead content of Jupiter. It will not, as Moon, separate from Jupiter, but will be within Jupiter, and it will be continually thrusting up these Earth-relics. And these Earth-relics will have to be animated as species-souls by the souls above.

And now you will remember what I have told you some years ago: that the human race on Jupiter will divide itself into those souls who have attained their Earth-goal, who will have attained the goal of Jupiter, and into those souls who will form a middle kingdom between the human kingdom and the animal kingdom on Jupiter. These latter will be Luciferic souls—Luciferic, merely spiritual. They will have their body below, and it will be a direct expression of their whole inner being, but they will be able to direct it only from outside. Two races, the good and the bad, will differentiate themselves from one another on Jupiter. This was stated years ago; today we wish to consider it more deeply.

A Venus-existence will follow that of Jupiter, and again there will be an adjustment through the further evolution of the Christ; but it is on Jupiter that man will realise what it means to be perfected only in his own ego, instead of making the whole Earth his concern. That is something he will have to experience through the whole course of the Jupiter cycle, for everything he has not permeated with Christ during his earthly existence may then appear before his spiritual sight.

Let us reflect from this point of view upon the words of Christ with which He sent His disciples out into the world to proclaim His Name, and in His Name to forgive sins. Why to forgive sins in His Name? Because the forgiveness of sins is connected with His Name. Sins can be blotted out and transformed into living life only if Christ can be united with our Earth-relics, if during our Earth-existence He is within us in the sense of the Pauline saying: "Not I, but Christ in me".

And wherever any religious denomination associates itself in its outer observances with this saying of Christ, in order to bring home to souls, again and again, all that is connected with Christ, we must seek this deeper meaning in it. When, in any religious denomination, one of Christ's servants speaks of the forgiveness of sins, as though by Christ's command, it means that with his words he forms a connection with the forgiveness of sins through Christ, and to the soul in need of comfort he says, in effect: "I have seen that you have developed a living relationship to Christ. You are uniting the objective sin and guilt, and the objective sin and guilt that will enter into your Earth-relics, with everything that Christ is for you. Because I have recognised that you have permeated yourself with Christ—therefore I dare say to you: your sins are forgiven."

Such words always mean that he who in any religious denomination speaks of the forgiveness of sins is convinced that the person in question has found a connection with Christ, that he wants to bear Christ in his heart and in his soul. Because of this he can properly give comfort when the other person comes to him conscious of guilt. "Christ will forgive you, and I am permitted to say to you that in His Name your sins are forgiven." Christ is the only forgiver of sins because He is the bearer of sins. He is the Being who gives life to human Earth-relics, and a wonderful link with Him is created when those who want to serve Him can give comfort in the words, "Your sins are forgiven", to those who show that in their inner being they feel a union with Christ. For it is like a fresh strengthening of the relationship to Christ when the soul realises: "I have understood my guilt and sins in such a way that it can permissibly be said to me that Christ takes them upon himself, works through them with his being." If the expression "the forgiveness of sins" is to be an expression of the truth, it must always carry an undertone which reminds the sinner of his bond with Christ, even if he does not form it anew. Between the soul and Christ there must be a bond so intense that the soul cannot be reminded of it often enough. And because the Christ is bound up with the objective sin and guilt of the human soul, the soul can best remind itself in daily life of its relationship to Christ by always remembering, at the moment of the forgiveness of sins, the presence of the Cosmic Christ in the Earth's existence.

Those who join Anthroposophy in the right spirit, and not merely in an external sense, can most assuredly become their own father confessors. Most assuredly through spiritual science they can learn to know Christ so intimately, and feel themselves so closely connected with Him, that they can be directly conscious of His spiritual presence. And when they have solemnly vowed themselves to Him as the Cosmic Principle, they can in spirit direct their confession to Him and in their silent meditation ask from Him the forgiveness of sins. But as long as men have not yet permeated themselves with spiritual science in this deep spiritual sense, we must look with understanding at what the "forgiveness of sins" signifies in the various religious observances of the world. Men will become spiritually freer and freer, and in this greater spiritual freedom their communion with Christ will become more and more a direct experience.

And there must be tolerance! A person who believes that through the deep inward understanding he has of the Spirit of the Mystery of Golgotha, the Christ, he can hold direct intercourse with the Christ, must look with understanding upon those who need the positive declarations of a confession of faith, and a minister of Christ to give them comfort with words, "Your sins are forgiven". On the other hand there should be tolerance on the part of those who see that there are men who can be independent. In earthly life this may be all an ideal, but the anthroposophist may at least look up to such an ideal.

I have spoken to you of spiritual secrets which make it

possible for men—even those who have absorbed much anthroposophical teaching—to look still more deeply into the whole nature of our being. I have spoken to you of the overcoming of human egoism, and of those things we must understand before we can have a right understanding of Karma. I have spoken to you of man in so far as he is not only an "I" being, but belongs to the whole Earth-existence and is thereby called to help forward the attainment of the divine aim appointed for the Earth. The Christ did not come into the world and pass through the Mystery of Golgotha in order that He might be something to each one of us in our egoism. It would be terrible if Christ were to be so understood that the words of Paul, "Not I, but Christ in me" served only to encourage a higher egoism. Christ died for the whole of humanity, for the humanity of the Earth. Christ became the central Spirit of the Earth, who has to save for the Earth the spiritual-earthly elements that flow out from man.

Nowadays one can read theological works—and those who have read them will bear me out—which assure us that certain theologians of the nineteenth and twentieth centuries have at last disposed of the popular mediaeval belief that Christ came to Earth in order to snatch the Earth from the devil, to snatch the Earth from Lucifer. Within modern theology there is an "enlightened" materialism which will not recognise itself as such but on the contrary imagines itself to be specially enlightened. It says: "In the dark Middle Ages people said that Christ appeared in the world because He had to snatch the Earth away from the devil." But the true explanation leads us back to this simple, popular belief. For everything on the Earth that is not set free by Christ belongs to Lucifer. All that is human in us, all that is more than what is merely confined in our ego, is ennobled, is made fruitful for the whole of humanity, when it is permeated with Christ.

And now, at the end of our considerations during the last few days, I would not like to conclude without saying these further words to each single one of the souls who are gathered together here:

Hope and confidence in the future of our work can dwell in our hearts, because we have endeavoured, from the very beginning, to fill what we had to say with the will of Christ. And this hope and confidence may allow us to say that our teaching is itself what Christ has wished to say to us, in fulfilment of His words: "I am with you always, even to the end of the Earth ages." We have wished to be mindful only of what comes from Him. And all that He has inspired us with, according to His promise, we want to take into our souls as our spiritual science. It is not because we feel our spiritual science to be imbued with any sort of Christian dogmatism that we regard it as Christian, but because, having Christ within us, we look on it as a revelation of the Christ in ourselves. I am therefore also convinced that the springing up of true spiritual science in those souls who want to receive, with us, our Christ-filled spiritual science will be fruitful for the whole of humanity, and especially for those who welcome these fruits.

Clairvoyant observation shows that much of what is good, spiritually good, in our Movement proceeds from those who have taken our Christian spiritual science into themselves, and then, having passed through the gate of death, send down to us the fruits of this Christian spiritual science. The Christian spiritual science which those souls have taken into themselves and are now sending down to us from the spiritual worlds is already living in us. For they do not keep it in their own karmic stream for the sake of their own perfecting: they can let it stream into those who want to receive it. Comfort and hope arise for our spiritual science when we know that our so-called "dead" are working with us.

In the second lecture we spoke about these things in a certain connection. But today, when we have come to the close of the course, I should like to add a personal word.

While I have been speaking to the Norrkoping Branch of our Society, I could not be other than conscious always of the spirit of one who was so closely connected with us here. The spirit of Frau Danielsen looks down like a good angel on all that this Branch wants to undertake. Hers also was a Christian spirit in the sense described, and the souls who knew her will never feel themselves separated from her. May that spirit hover as guardian-spirit over this Branch. Most willingly and surely will it do so if the souls who work in this Branch receive it. With these words, spoken from the depths of my heart, I close these lectures, and I hope that we shall continue to work together on the spiritual path we have embraced.

CONCERNING THE TRANSCRIPTS OF THE LECTURES

From Rudolf Steiner's autobiography *Mein Lebensgang (My Life)*, Chapter 35, 1925. It was subsequently published in English, *Rudolf Steiner, An Autobiography*, 2nd Edition, Multimedia Pub. Corp., New York, 1980.

Two consequences of my anthroposophical activity are the books which were made accessible to the general public and an extensive series of lecture courses which were initially intended for private circulation and were available only to members of the Theosophical (later Anthroposophical) Society. The transcripts of the latter were taken down—some more accurately than others—during my lectures. But time did not permit me to undertake their correction. I, for my part, would have preferred spoken word to remain spoken word, but the Members were in favour of private publication of the Courses. And so it came about. If I had had time to correct the transcripts, the reservation "For Members Only" need not have been made from the very first. Now it has been dropped for over a year.

Here in "My Life" it is above all necessary to explain how the two—the publications in general and in private circulation—are accommodated in my elaboration of Anthroposophy.

Whoever wishes to pursue my own inner conflict and toil in my effort to introduce Anthroposophy to contemporary thought, must do so with the aid of the works in general circulation which include analysis of all forms of cognition of this age. Therein also lies that which crystallised within me in "spiritual vision" and from which came into existence the structure of Anthroposophy, even if imperfect in many respects.

Apart from this obligation to construct Anthroposophy and thereby to serve only that which ensues when communications from the Spirit World are to be transmitted to modern civilisation, the need also arose to meet the claims which were manifested within the Membership as a compulsion, a yearning of the soul.

Above all, many Members were greatly disposed to hearing the Gospels and the scriptural content of the Bible presented in an anthroposophical light. Courses were requested which were to examine such revelations to humanity.

Internal courses were held to meet this requirement. At these lectures only Members were present who were initiated in Anthroposophy. It was possible to speak to them as to those well versed in Anthroposophy. The delivery of these internal lectures was such as simply could not be communicated in written works intended for the general public.

In these closed circles I was able to discuss subjects which I would have had to present quite differently if they had been intended for a general public from the very first.

Thus in the duality of the public and private works there actually exists something of two-fold diverse origin. The wholly public writings are a result of that which struggled and toiled within me; in the private publications, the Society struggles and toils with me. I listen to the vibrations within the Soul-life of the Membership and within my own being and the tone of the lectures arises from what I hear there.

Nowhere has even the slightest mention of anything been

made which does not proceed from the substance of Anthroposophy. No concessions can be made to any prejudices or presentiments existing within the Membership. Whoever reads these private publications can accept them as a true representation of anthroposophical conviction. Thus when petitions became more urgent, the ruling as to the private circulation of these publications within the Membership could be amended without any hesitation. Any errors occurring in transcripts which I have not been able to revise will however have to be tolerated.

The right to pass judgement on the content of any such private publication is nevertheless reserved to those possessing the prerequisite to do so. For the great majority of these publications, this is *at least* an anthroposophical knowledge of man and the universe, in so far as its essence is presented in Anthroposophy, and of "the history of anthroposophy" such as it is derived from communications from the Spirit-World.

Complete Edition of the works of Rudolf Steiner in German, published by the Rudolf Steiner Verlag, Dornach, Switzerland, by whom all rights are reserved.

Writings

1. Works written between 1883 and 1925
2. Essays and articles written between 1882 and 1925
3. Letters, drafts, manuscripts, fragments, verses, inscriptions, meditative sayings, etc.

Lectures

1. Public Lectures
2. Lectures to Members of the Anthroposophical Society on general anthroposophical subjects.
   Lectures to Members on the history of the Anthroposophical Movement and Anthroposophical Society
3. Lectures and Courses on special branches of work:
   Art: Eurythmy, Speech and Drama, Music, Visual Arts, History of
   Art
   Education
   Medicine and Therapy
   Science
   Sociology and the Threefold Social Order
   Lectures given to Workmen at the Goetheanum

The total number of lectures amount to some six thousand, shorthand reports of which are available in the case of the great majority.

Reproductions and Sketches

Paintings in water colour, drawings, coloured diagrams, Eurythmy forms, etc.

When the Edition is complete the total number of volumes, each of a considerable size, will amount to several hundreds. A full and detailed Bibliographical Survey, with subjects, dates and places where the lectures were given is available. All the volumes can be obtained from the Rudolf Steiner Press in London as well as directly from the Rudolf Steiner Verlag, Dornach, Switzerland.